A Genius in His Way

A Genius in His Way

The Art of Cable's *Old Creole Days*

Alice Hall Petry

Rutherford • Madison • Teaneck
Fairleigh Dickinson University Press
London and Toronto: Associated University Presses

Associated University Presses
440 Forsgate Drive
Cranbury, NJ 08512

Associated University Presses
25 Sicilian Avenue
London WC1A 2QH, England

Associated University Presses
P.O. Box 488, Port Credit
Mississauga, Ontario
Canada L5G 4M2

The paper used in this publication meets the requirements
of the American National Standard for Permanence of Paper
for Printed Library Materials Z39.48-1984.

Library of Congress Cataloging-in-Publication Data

Petry, Alice Hall, 1951–
    A genius in his way.

    Bibliography: p.
    Includes index.
    1. Cable, George Washington, 1844–1925. Old Creole
days. 2. New Orleans (La.) in literature. 3. French
Americans in literature. 4. Creoles in literature.
I. Title.
PS1244.063P48   1988   813'.4   87-45574
ISBN 0-8386-3320-X (alk. paper)

Printed in the United States of America

For My Parents
James B. and Elizabeth K. Hall

Contents

Acknowledgments

I wish to thank the staff of the Fairleigh Dickinson University Press, and in particular Harry Keyishian and Walter Cummins; Louis D. Rubin, Jr., of *Southern Literary Journal,* for granting me permission to reprint (in slightly modified form) my essay on "Jean-ah Poquelin"; Robert L. Phillips; Alan Gribben; and Steen H. Spove, editor of *Studies in Short Fiction,* whose advice has proved invaluable. Finally, special thanks go to George Monteiro of Brown University. Dr. Monteiro's impact on American literary scholarship—both through his own extensive research and his encouragement of so many younger scholars—has been profound.

A Genius in His Way

Introduction

WRITING about George Washington Cable (1844–1925) in 1967, Griffith T. Pugh assessed his current status in American letters: "Cable has not been re-discovered, for he was never lost sight of. Nor has he been reinterpreted, for, except for an occasional mistaken or silly notion, he seems not to have been misinterpreted."[1] That situation was significantly altered in the early 1980s, when the centennial publication of Cable's novel *The Grandissimes* (1880) spawned a flurry of studies, proving that, if readers had "never lost sight of" Cable, they also had never really noticed him for most of this century. A novel that had been relegated to the dubious realm of "formerly popular" works is now regarded as one of the finest achievements in American literature. But the short stories, those "quaint, pathetic, and humorous tales" that Richard Chase so handily dismissed in *The American Novel and Its Tradition,*[2] had not enjoyed a comparable renaissance. The story collection *Old Creole Days* (1879) still exists in a critical limbo. Having generally been passed over in the twentieth century's explosion of literary scholarship, *Old Creole Days* is best known to literature specialists as a title on graduate program reading lists; only occasionally do its stories (usually "Belles Demoiselles Plantation" or the novella *Madame Delphine*) appear in anthologies of the American short story or in textbooks devoted to Southern literature.[3] And part and parcel with the disinclination to read Cable is the disinclination to approach his writings as works of art. As Pugh's remarks imply, there seems to be a widespread and tenacious assumption that there is nothing in Cable which could possibly be misinterpreted—that he is so superficial, so transparent, so "simple" if you will, that his writings are not conducive to serious critical study. Nothing could be further from the truth. In his own day Cable was regarded as possessing "the most exquisite literary and artistic gifts that any American writer of fiction . . . has been endowed with since Hawthorne"; his skill in characterization was compared to that of Flaubert; he was perceived as belonging to "the literary family of Tourguéneff"; and he was praised for an "uninvaded individuality" tinged with a "rare whiff of Victor Hugo."[4] Charles Dudley Warner saw Cable's short fiction as "the solution of all the pother we have recently got into about the realistic and the ideal schools in fiction," for Cable's art "steps in . . . to make literature" out of faithful renderings of low life.[5] In

1884, a list of "Forty Immortals" in the *Critic* ranked Cable ahead of Samuel Clemens, and in 1899 Cable appeared tenth on a list of the greatest living American writers in *Literature*.[6] Indeed, Charles DeKay spoke for many in 1879 when he declared that Cable "is no mere talented writer; he is a genius in his way."[7] In light of this, it is rather startling to find that in the twentieth century the tendency has been to approach Cable's writings—if at all—from narrow, fundamentally nonliterary angles, such as his use of dialect ("George W. Cable's Theory and Use of Folk Speech") or his stance on sociopolitical or cultural matters ("Cable and the Creoles"),[8] and most of these analyses have focused on *The Grandissimes* rather than on the short stories. A handful of scholars—Arlin Turner, Louis D. Rubin, Jr., and Philip Butcher—certainly have recognized the artistry of the short stories; but their excellent discussions of the tales have been necessarily limited by the simple fact that each man wrote a general critical biography of Cable, a broad survey of his life and work that could not afford to devote the time or space necessary for a full appreciation of *Old Creole Days*.[9] As a result, a large gap exists in Cable scholarship, and it is this gap that *A Genius in His Way* seeks to fill. By drawing upon the observations of Turner, Rubin, and Butcher, as well as those of essayists such as Howard W. Fulweiler, Donald A. Ringe, and Etienne de Planchard, I offer detailed, systematic analyses of the eight tales of *Old Creole Days*: *Madame Delphine*, "Café des Exilés," "Belles Demoiselles Plantation," "Posson Jone'," "Jean-ah Poquelin," " 'Tite Poulette," " 'Sieur George," and "Madame Délicieuse." My ultimate purposes are simply stated: to demonstrate that Cable's contemporaries were accurate in their appraisal of him as a literary artist, a "genius," and to restore him to his rightful place as one of the finest short story writers in American literature.

To these ends, I have avoided discussing matters of biography, economics, politics, and so on, except as they illuminate the artistry of the stories; anyone seeking information on such matters should consult the studies of Turner, Rubin, Butcher, or Kjell Ekström, whose 1950 doctoral dissertation (Upsala, Sweden) offers a general introduction to Cable's life and the milieu in which he worked. By the same token, I have not sought to offer extensive definitions of terms that would be familiar to most students of Cable. It may be helpful to note, however, that I use the term "Creole"—as did Cable—to refer to a Caucasian, usually upper-class native New Orleanian of French ancestry. The few times Cable speaks of Creoles of Spanish ancestry (as in "Café des Exilés"), he is usually careful to emphasize their non-Gallic background ("Spanish Creoles").[10] The "Code Noir" ("Black Code") was a system of laws first introduced into Louisiana in 1724. Designed to define the legal status and civil rights of whites and blacks, the Code Noir eventually crystallized into an elaborate system of racial segregation, the effects of which were not seriously challenged until the civil rights movement of the 1960s.[11] A third term, "local color," rarely appears in this study, simply because it has been so overused that it is practically meaningless. I use it in a slightly pejorative sense to mean those "picturesque" details of local life that would be unfamiliar, and probably intriguing, to a non-Southern audience.[12] I should also mention that I have avoided the temptation to discuss *The Grandissimes,* or to present that masterpiece as a standard by which to judge the tales. As the eight chapters in this book suggest, *Old Creole Days* can stand on its own merits, and several of the tales—"Belles Demoiselles Plantation," "Jean-ah Poquelin," " 'Sieur George," and "Posson Jone' "—are probably among the finest short stories in American literature.

The exceptional merit of these stories is readily apparent from my purely artistic approach to Cable. Likewise readily discernible are the various techniques and themes that he derived from his considerable knowledge of Western (especially English and American) literature, and that in several instances he developed into veritable trademarks of his own fiction. Cable was exceptionally well-read: Kjell Ekström points out that the names of over fifty novelists, essayists, and poets appear in the eighty-eight "Drop Shot" columns Cable wrote for the New Orleans *Picayune,* including Bacon, Milton, Tennyson, Byron, Scott, and Longfellow.[13] But the names of four authors figure most prominently in Cable's fiction and private correspondence: Edgar Allan Poe, Nathaniel Hawthorne, Charles Dickens, and William Shakespeare. These would appear to be most responsible for the evolution of Cable's style as a writer of fiction.

An important element of that style is what one might term the utilization of dense, organic, highly evocative language. At times, reading *Old Creole Days* is like reading poetry, and not without reason. Although well-read in all genres, Cable reported that he "thought most on poetry," and in fact he published more than sixty poems of his own composition, "many of them nonsense rhymes concocted of puns, conundrums, parodies, and countless novelties of thought and method."[14] It is a description that calls to mind Cable's fellow Southerner, Poe, whose acrostics (e.g., "A Valentine") and musically evocative verse ("The Bells") would have appealed greatly to a man of Cable's temperament. Like Poe, Cable had a rational turn of mind coupled with a predilection for the intangible, the unknown, even the whimsical; it is an unusual combination that may help explain their rather eclectic personal and fictional interests (e.g., unorthodox sexual conduct and mathematics) as well as the rich musicality of their writing styles—Cable himself praised Poe's "bewildering harmony" and "marvelous melody"[15]—that at times may seem to sacrifice clear meaning on the altar of sound. Cable had studied Poe at home as a boy, and acknowledged readily Poe's influence on his work;[16] not surprisingly, there are numerous echoes of specific works of Poe throughout *Old Creole Days*. "Belles Demoiselles Plantation," for instance, is enhanced significantly by its transparent connections with "The Conqueror Worm" and "The Fall of the House of Usher."

Poe's example may also have been one of the factors in Cable's penchant for using highly evocative charactonyms. In "Jean-ah Poquelin," for example, Cable's use of the name "Little White" for one of the characters is deliberately confusing, and as such it contributes enormously to the presentation of that story's themes. If "Little White" lacks the ingenuity of the anagrammatic "*Imp* of the Perverse" / *Pym,* or the doubling effect of *Fortun*ato / Mon*tresor* (The Cask of Amontillado"),[17] it nonetheless reflects a Poesque fondness for wordplay and his appreciation of the symbolic potential of the well-chosen charactonym. Somewhat more common in Cable's fiction is what one might term a Dickensian approach to charactonyms. Cable adored Dickens: he is known to have read *The Pickwick Papers* by 1865; he had become quite familiar with the Dickens canon before he began his own career; and he freely admitted to literary historian Fred Lewis Pattee that Dickens had been a major influence on his work.[18] Dickens, of course, used charactonyms that convey phonetically the personalities, physical size, or social status of his characters; even out of context, the very sounds of such names as Pip, Peggotty, Dora, Ebenezer Scrooge, and Mr. Murdstone suggest the nature of the people themselves, and Cable uses the same technique with good effect with such charactonyms as 'Tite Poulette, Koppig, Dr. Mossy, and Kookoo. Cable sometimes also uses the blatantly symbolic charactonyms typical of religious parables and allegories. As a lifelong student of the Bible and devoted Sunday school teacher, Cable was well aware of the capacities of certain names to elevate stories from pure fiction to didactic literature. Hence, for example, the name Olive in *Madame Delphine* for a girl of mixed blood (olive-skinned) whose marriage to a white man will be a source of personal and societal peace (represented traditionally by an olive branch).

Generally speaking, the charactonyms in Cable tell us much about the characters themselves, but surprisingly often they conceal far more than they reveal. Pseudonyms, nicknames, and assumed or imposed titles (e.g., "Madame" for an unmarried woman) are rampant in *Old Creole Days*. They are perhaps the most obvious manifestation of a much larger pattern in Cable's fiction: unclear or uncertain identity. Very much like Poe, Cable utilizes literal concealment (masks, peepholes), subdued lighting, and false names to hide the true identities of his characters; also like Poe, he does not use this technique as an end in itself. Cable presents uncertain identity as a dramatic result of the harsh socioeconomic and legal realities of nineteenth-century New Orleans—especially of the Code Noir, which was known to declare blue-eyed blonds as legal blacks, which led guilt-ridden couples to regard their illicit liaisons as de facto marriages, and which forced desperate women to disavow their light-skinned biological children rather than see them subjected to discrimination. If at times Cable's characters themselves seem uncertain about their own identities, it is precisely because they must function in a society that twists or denies the traditional sources of identity—one's given name, family background, race, economic status, education, and religious faith. Cable's fondness for imposed or assumed identities, as well as for ironically appropriate given names, may also owe much to the precedent of Nathaniel Hawthorne, one of the authors Cable cites frequently in his "Drop Shot" columns,[19] and the writer with whom Cable was compared most consistently in his own day. The unclear identities and multifaceted, often ironic charactonyms that are so common in the Hawthorne canon—Young Goodman Brown and his wife Faith attend Black Sabbath; the photographer Holgrave proves to be the last of the Maules in *The House of the Seven Gables*—show a clear affinity with Cable's practice in *Old Creole Days*.

The confusion and uncertainty engendered by the complex socioeconomic and legal situation that he depicts in his fiction led Cable to develop a distinctive character type: the benevolent voyeur. Broadly speaking, this is a character who, while physically concealed, studies those around him in an attempt to determine the truth of their situation (hence "voyeur"). For the most part, the individuals he chooses to observe are helpless, innocent, and usually female; and far from being malicious, he is deeply concerned over their personal well-being (hence "benevolent"). He may or may not become personally involved with those he observes; but whatever the case, the benevolent voyeur almost always is unable to avert—or even to warn them about—some tragedy. He watches them suffer, feeling acute anguish for being unable to help. The benevolent voyeur is a Hawthornesque element (consider Miles Coverdale in *The Blithedale Romance* and Giovanni Guasconti in "Rappaccini's Daughter"), but Cable uses it far more frequently than Hawthorne. Indeed, it is a virtual trademark of his fiction, and its presence in a Cable story generally foreshadows tragedy.

The uncertain legal and social standings and the concomitant unclear identities that the benevolent voyeur attempts to fathom have a textual counterpart in *Old Creole Days*: semantic ambiguity. For the most part, this takes the form of unclear antecedents. As one sees so frequently in the fiction of both Hawthorne and Poe, words such as "them," "this," "they," and "it" frequently can refer to several different antecedents; even ostensibly precise personal pronouns such as "he" and "she" may refer to more than one person. The reader is understandably confused; as such, he is able to share (albeit to a limited degree) in the confusion experienced by the Cable characters themselves. Cable further seems to be encouraging this type of reader participation by experimenting with narrative technique—something he has in common with a contemporary who traditionally has over-shadowed him, Henry James. In "Café des Exilés," for example, Cable utilizes an unreliable narrator who presents his material at second hand; the reader never knows whether to trust the narrator, any more than the characters in the story know if they can trust one another. In " 'Tite Poul-ette," the story is told from the point of view of an outsider who does not understand the nuances of the situation he is observing. No reader could blame the Dutchman for wishing to help the unfortunate mother and daughter who live across the street, and no reader could fail to be shocked when his well-meant attempt to intervene on their behalf nearly cause the death of this benevolent voyeur. Occasionally Cable utilizes a narrator who is almost impossible to differentiate from the author himself, as he acts as a chatty (but ultimately quite serious) tour guide leading the reader through the less familiar districts of exotic New Orleans—a narrative technique quite reminiscent of Hawthorne's presentation of Rome in *The Marble Faun*. Or the narrator may be presented as a historian who researches his stories in city newspapers and public archives; ostensibly he is an antiquarian who simply is presenting his material to the reader as if it were a kind of fictionalized history lesson, when in fact that material has a strong moral dimension. This presentation of *Madame Delphine*—complete with a schol-arly footnote advising the reader to "See gazettes of the period" (15)—is of course reminiscent of the stance Hawthorne assumes in "The Custom House" and *The Scarlet Letter*. The exceptional richness and variety of narrative technique in *Old Creole Days* suggest the seriousness with which Cable approached his material; he is clearly no mere recorder of charming local color seeking simply to entertain a passive reader. At the same time, this experimentation suggests that Cable, like William Faulkner after him, recognized fully that the complexity of his material necessitated a diversity of narrative stances. No single angle or approach could do justice to the confusing, ambiguous world of early-nineteenth-century New Orleans.

The many sources of confusion in that world—and, hence, in Cable's fiction—might lead one to expect an extremely challenging reading experi-ence, but this is the case only rarely. For the most part, Cable effectively guides his reader's response to his work by utilizing two interrelated tech-niques: private homes are used to symbolize the personal situations of their residents, and buildings (especially public ones) often serve as gauges of socioeconomic change. Both the doomed plantation of the Belles Demoi-selles and the rotting mansion of Jean-ah Poquelin, for example, are em-blems of the families with which they are associated (currently and historically) and, more specifically, of the present male heads of their house-holds. One is reminded immediately of Poe's House of Usher, Miss Havisham's mansion in Dickens's *Great Expectations*, and Hawthorne's House of Pyncheon. Similarly, the deteriorating neighborhoods and crumbling shops in *Madame Delphine* and " 'Sieur George" are a Dickensian motif that helps the reader to respond to early-nineteenth-century New Orleans as a world undergoing painful and sometimes disastrous socioeconomic change and cultural upheaval, rather than as just a quaint and picturesque Southern seaport. In many ways Cable was as uncompromising a realist as William Dean Howells, Dickens (as in *Oliver Twist*), or even Stephen Crane, whose vivid representations of life in the poor districts of New York City in the 1890s may well owe much to the example of *Old Creole Days.*

Cable's much-analyzed phonetic representations of the various languages and dialects of polyglot early-nineteenth-century New Orleans are a manifestation of his fidelity to realism; but they also point to another source of Cable's fictional art: drama. Perhaps too much has been made of Cable's being fired from his job as a newspaper reporter for refusing to review a local play; his alleged opposition to drama on religious grounds should be put into proper perspective.[20] It is true that his mother Rebecca Boardman, an Indianian of New England Puritan stock, and his first wife Louise Bartlett (d. 1904) were opposed to the theater on religious grounds; but it also seems clear that they differentiated between attending plays and simply reading them as literature—and there is ample evidence that Cable indulged in the latter. Arlin Turner notes that Cable had studied Shakespeare on his own at home,[21] and there seem to be echoes of Shakespeare's plays throughout his fiction, including similarities between Père Jerome of *Madame Delphine,* and the Friar Laurence of *Romeo and Juliet.* As will be seen in the analysis of " 'Sieur George," Cable also seems to have had considerable knowledge of the life and writings of Molière. But even where specific correlations cannot be drawn between Cable's stories and various plays, the influence of drama is everywhere evident in his fiction. The heavy reliance on dialogue makes "Posson Jone' " read almost like a play; dumb shows are used to excellent advantage in " 'Sieur George," "Belles Demoiselles Plantation," and " 'Tite Poulette"; and the spare initial presentation of characters coupled with well-defined settings render the stories of *Old Creole Days* highly theatrical. Whether Cable borrowed these techniques directly from playwrights, or indirectly through Hawthorne (as Turner argues[22]) or the histrionic Mr. Poe, the fact remains that Cable's stories are often strikingly similar to dramas. Indeed, Cable's affinity for drama was so powerful that just four years after the publication of *Old Creole Days* he actually began to attend plays, despite his family's misgivings. His reaction to an 1883 Broadway dramatization of Dickens's *Cricket on the Hearth* hardly betokens a strict Presbyterian's scorn for the wicked theater: " 'If it isn't as pure & sweet & refreshing & proper a diversion as spending the same length of time over a pretty, sweet, good story-book, then I'm a dunce. . . . I feel . . . as if I had had a bath in pure, cool water. I am fitted anew for working & loving & doing good. I thank God for the pleasure I have had. . . . ' "[23] Thanks to this belated discovery of the power of live performance, Cable became quite receptive to the dramatization of his stories for the theater or for silent motion pictures. And although part of his motive was financial, for the most part it was, ironically, moral. Contrary to his family's opposition to drama on religious grounds, Cable came to understand that the theater was a potential agent for ennobling the masses.

And Cable was, after all, an insistently moral writer. Part of Hawthorne's appeal for him was the elder writer's mastery of elements with which Cable felt comfortable. Arlin Turner sees " 'Sieur George," for example, as being Hawthornesque in its "location of the action in a hazily defined past, real in atmosphere rather than circumstantial details, and [its] reliance on hints and speculation instead of direct assertion."[24] But in fact Cable's more obvious and important kinships with Hawthorne have less to do with technique than with moral stance. Both Hawthorne and Cable approached spiritual matters from the perspective of humanitarianism rather than the dogma of a particular religious sect. Cable was remarkably open-minded for someone raised in a nineteenth-century Presbyterian household, and despite his lifelong activities in the church (both Presbyterian and Congregational),[25] he had increasingly less conviction that organized religion could be an instrument of social reform. Organized religion in the South, after all, was an eloquent defender of racism and slavery—matters the outraged Cable attacked openly in *Madame Delphine*. For Cable as for Hawthorne, it was one's personal conduct and beliefs—what Cable termed " 'right methods of thought and inquiry; intellectual humility and integrity' "[26]—that determined one's goodness, not membership in a vocal, exclusive, self-serving church. It is not surprising that both authors were dismayed by the nineteenth-century impulse to denigrate the "heart" (faith and good works) in favor of the "head" (intellectualism, technology, commerce); or that they shared the conviction that one's personal and communal history—including the deeply instilled, misguided dictates of what Cable termed the "cobwebby" church[27]—could constitute an intolerable psychological burden; or that they both felt deep empathy for sensitive individuals (especially women) who try to survive with dignity in a hostile and frequently morally ambiguous world. Hawthorne and Cable both focus, for example, on "fallen" women who endure by virtue of their compassion, intelligence, and common sense, and who seek a better life far away (read "a good marriage") for their illegitimate daughters. The moral maze of Puritan Boston that Hester Prynne was compelled to navigate was no less intimidating and potentially destructive than that faced by Madame John (" 'Tite Poulette") and Madame Delphine in predominantly Roman Catholic early-nineteenth-century New Orleans, and both authors condemn their societies far more than the women themselves. A self-righteous, ill-formed, inflexible interpretation of the Scriptures that hurts those who will not, or can not, conform to social norms particularly appalled both men. For them, a "true Christian" may—like Hester Prynne or Hilda the Dove, like Posson Jone' or Jules St.-Ange—be someone who makes mistakes, defies the norm, or simply is unable to determine how to behave in a difficult situation; what matters is that he tries to conduct his life with dignity and compassion. Further, he may not come to a full realization of his status as a true Christian until his personal life is at its lowest ebb. It is a situation quite reminiscent of the fiction of Flannery O'Connor, and in fact it may be argued that Cable is an unrecognized but absolutely vital influence on Miss O'Connor's mind and art. The self-serving distortions of the Scriptures by so many of her characters, the violence, the confused identities, unclear antecedents, careful presentation of Southern dialect, multifaceted charactonyms, symbolic buildings, mistrust of intellectualism, benevolent voyeurs, and even the recurrent bird imagery—all are Cablesque elements that are clearly evident in the fiction of this most overtly religious writer in twentieth-century American literature. And although Cable no doubt would have felt uncomfortable with the insistent Roman Catholicism of Miss O'Connor's work, it is nonetheless true that both authors never equated the fundamental teachings of the Bible with the dictates of organized religion in its often imperfect contemporary form. Each author saw the Bible as a rich source book, both as an inspiring guide for moral conduct in a seemingly chaotic world, and as a repository of symbols, images, ideas, and stories that could be utilized to impart a didactic dimension to their fiction. Each author recognized that a short story could be simultaneously an entertaining tale, a document of social commentary, and a modern-day religious parable enlivened and enriched by humor, irony, a keen eye for detail, and a dense and poetic writing style redolent of the King James Bible. Perhaps even more than Hawthorne,[28] it is Cable who seems to have offered Miss O'Connor the fictional models for her extraordinary short stories and novels.

The moral dimension of Cable's fiction is so powerful that it is remarkable that his stories do not read essentially like fictionalized Sunday school lessons—a criticism leveled at so many of Miss O'Connor's stories. It was a very real danger for a man who conducted adult Bible study classes and taught Sunday school throughout his life, and he took pains not to alienate his readership by creating what he termed " 'goody-goody' " characters. As he wrote to William Dean Howells in 1881, " 'there is no sound reason why goodness should not be artistically wrought. It is only our wretched ideas of goodness that make such walking mummies as blast the fond parental hopes of most female and many male fictionists.' "[29] One potential walking mummy is the protagonist of " 'Tite Poulette": Kristian sounds—and sometimes behaves—like his namesake in Bunyan's *Pilgrim's Progress,* but Cable goes to great lengths to undercut his allegorical "goody-goody" dimension, even giving him an unflattering surname. "Koppig" is Dutch for "head-

strong" or "obstinate," and its lumbering sound nicely counters the reader's
tendency to see any well-meaning character named "Kristian" as somehow
angelic. Soon after the completion of *Old Creole Days* Cable's impulse to
sermonize became an increasingly salient feature of his fiction, and *Century*
editor Richard Watson Gilder ultimately would urge him to reread
Hawthorne to see how didactic material could be presented with artisitic
grace.[30] But during the creation of *Old Creole Days* in the 1870s, Cable was
still able to strike a kind of balance between the two—a balance that rather
often tipped in favor of artistry. Indeed, the impact of even the most
transparent allegories (such as "Belles Demoiselles Plantation") tends to be
lost in our enjoyment of the stories themselves, and in a way one might not
wish it otherwise: even if they are not always quite successful as documents
of religious truth, the stories of *Old Creole Days* are often outstanding
examples of fictional artistry.

That artistry is particularly evident, I believe, in my story-by-story
approach to *Old Creole Days*. My decision to devote one chapter to each of
the eight tales, rather than to particular themes or techniques, is based upon
the conviction that a story's artistry is most palpable when it is examined as
a unit. To pull a series of elements out of their proper fictional contexts
would fragment the stories and perhaps obscure the subtleties of Cable's
style and technique. Further, to devote a chapter to, say, Cable's use of the
benevolent voyeur would involve making sweeping generalizations that
might not be applicable to much of his fiction, and it would increase the
likelihood that Cable's less rewarding efforts, such as "Café des Exilés" or
"Madame Délicieuse," might be slighted. I must add that no attempt has
been made to standardize the lengths of the eight chapters. Those stories
that require fuller treatment as a result of their length or complexity have
received it.

Throughout this study I follow the text of the 1889 edition of *Old Creole
Days* published by Charles Scribner's Sons, New York; all page references
are to this edition. The first edition (1879) of the collection did not include
Madame Delphine; but as Fred Lewis Pattee points out, this novella, "despite
its length and its separate publication, is a short story belonging to the *Old
Creole Days* group,"[31] and in fact it has been included in the collection since
1883. It should also be noted that I discuss the stories in the exact order in
which they appear in the 1889 edition. When *Old Creole Days* was first
published in 1879, the stories were arranged in the order in which they were
published in *Scribner's Monthly Magazine* and *Appleton's Journal,* but with
"Belles Demoiselles Plantation" and " 'Tite Poulette" transposed. In the
revised edition of *Old Creole Days* published in 1883, Cable took the advice
of Hjalmar H. Boyesen and arranged for the collection to begin with
Madame Delphine and to close with "Madame Délicieuse," which both men
felt were the strongest pieces in the volume.[32] The 1889 edition retains this

revised arrangement, as do virtually all subsequent editions of *Old Creole Days*. I must also note that the 1889 edition is surprisingly free of typographical errors. The few I have encountered (such as "wdage" for "wadge" [watch] in "Café des Exilés") have been silently corrected. I have avoided using "[sic]"; as devotees of Cable realize, what appear at first glance to be misspelled words are actually his phonetic renderings of dialect. I also have indicated in the notes any significant revisions of the original texts of the stories, and I have kept to a minimum the cross-references between chapters.

1

"Dey's Quadroons": Love versus the Code Noir in *Madame Delphine*

IT was one of the more poignant developments of Cable's career that the novella *Madame Delphine* (1881) was written in response to an anonymous quadroon's complaint that his story "'Tite Poulette" (1874) begged the agonizing question of miscegenation in nineteenth-century New Orleans. By having the story's protagonist, the quadroon Madame John, suddenly reveal that her octoroon "daughter" was in fact Spanish (and therefore, as a Caucasian, legally able to marry her Dutch lover), Cable effectively skirted the whole issue of miscegenation and severely compromised the impact of what could have been one of the masterpieces of *Old Creole Days*. "[T]ell the inmost truth of it," urged the reader. "The girl was her own daughter; but like many and many a real quadroon mother, as you surely know, Madame John perjured her own soul to win for her child a legal and honorable alliance with the love-mate and life-mate of her choice." Cable vowed to retell the story in a more "truthful" fashion,[1] and seven years after the publication of "'Tite Poulette," *Madame Delphine* began to appear serially in *Scribner's Monthly Magazine* (May–July 1881). Cable himself was well pleased with it: "I have a notion I shall always be glad I wrote it," he remarked in the 1896 preface to the novella,[2] and throughout his long and prolific career he persisted in feeling it was his best story. But Cable's pride in *Madame Delphine* stemmed not solely from the psychological satisfaction of being honest about the plight of those of mixed blood. In the exploration of this sensitive social issue, Cable had faced in *Madame Delphine* a series of artistic challenges not presented by any of the other tales in *Old Creole Days*: at eighty pages, it is more than twice as long as any of the other stories; it offers an unprecedented number of individualized characters; and it seeks to examine the issue of miscegenation through three discrete but related approaches—the genetic, the legal, and the spiritual.[3] Further, *Madame Delphine* shows Cable skillfully handling the techniques and motifs that collectively are virtually his artistic trademark, including the strong opening, unclear identities, and trenchant irony. If *Madame Delphine* is not so successful as, say, "Jean-ah Poquelin," "Posson Jone'," or "'Sieur George," it nevertheless is an insistently Cablesque work that serves as the ideal introductory tale of *Old Creole Days*—a status it first acquired in the collection's 1883 edition, and held thereafter.

Cable's strong suit was always the opening of a story. Compressed into only one or two medium-length paragraphs is information vital for the understanding of plot, character, and theme, presented with an acute sensitivity to the nuances of diction and tone; and although the unusual length of *Madame Delphine* necessitated a corresponding expansion of the opening, it still is perfect for Cable's novella:

> A few steps from the St. Charles Hotel, in New Orleans, brings you to and across Canal Street, the central avenue of the city, and to that corner where the flower-women sit at the inner and outer edges of the arcaded sidewalk, and make the air sweet with their fragrant merchandise. The crowd—and if it is near the time of the carnival it will be great—will follow Canal Street. (1)

As Robert O. Stephens remarks in his 1979 essay, "Cable's *Madame Delphine* and the Compromise of 1877," the use of "the intimate second-person point of view" tends to pull the reader into the story.[4] He becomes a virtual character, part of the community that permitted the existence of the Code Noir and its institutionalized mistreatment of the quadroon Madame Delphine and her daughter Olive. This is of special importance in that Cable was quite conscious of writing for a Northern audience—an audience whose failure to challenge the Code Noir made them virtual accessories to the injustices perpetrated by it in the South. It is no accident that Cable begins the story "a few steps from the St. Charles Hotel" rather than from a private residence, or that the narrator is being posited as a type of tour guide, or that "flower-women" are strategically situated so as to "make the air sweet with their fragrant merchandise": this is the "picturesque" New Orleans that would be most familiar, most appealing, to a Northern tourist who might be staying at the hotel, and who might be part of that crowd at carnival time. The introductory paragraph, then, is calculated to be as charming and serene as New Orleans would appear to the eyes of a Northern tourist; but Cable immediately undercuts the superficial attractiveness of the scene with the first word of the second paragraph:

> But you turn, instead, into the quiet, narrow way which a lover of Creole antiquity, in fondness for a romantic past, is still prone to call the Rue Royale. You will pass a few restaurants, a few auction-rooms, a few furniture warehouses, and will hardly realize that you have left behind

you the activity and clatter of a city of merchants before you find yourself
in a region of architectural decrepitude, where an ancient and foreign-
seeming domestic life, in second stories, over-hangs the ruins of a former
commercial prosperity, and upon every thing has settled down a long
sabbath of decay. The vehicles in the street are few in number, and are
merely passing through; the stores are shrunken into shops; you see here
and there, like a patch of bright mould, the stall of that significant fungus,
the Chinaman. Many great doors are shut and clamped and grown gray
with cobweb; many street windows are nailed up; half the balconies are
begrimed and rust-eaten, and many of the humid arches and alleys which
characterize the older Franco-Spanish piles of stuccoed brick betray a
squalor almost oriental. (1–2)

The word "But" signals the transition: we permit the tour-guide narrator to
direct us out of the beaten path, and into a neighborhood comparatively
déclassé. Cable posits it as a physical journey, but the details he provides
make it quite clear that this is also a sociocultural and psychological journey
into the less appealing aspects of New Orleans—the dark underside of a
picturesque society. The reference to the "lover of Creole antiquity" who
harbors a "fondness for a romantic past" has, then, a double edge. On the
most fundamental level, Cable is speaking of the appreciation of New
Orleans's colorful past, which he shared with many others; but on a more
profound level, he is acknowledging the impossibility of clinging to a
romantic past so as to deny the harsh realities of the present: "fondness" was
occasionally used by Cable in its archaic sense, "foolishness."[5] The discrepancy between the "romantic past" and the harsh present is palpable in the
details Cable provides: the triple use of "a few" suggests the fragmented
quality of a neighborhood in decline, and the "auction-rooms" and "furniture warehouses" further indicate that the area residents are selling off or
storing the relics of that romantic past in order to maintain their current
tenuous lifestyle—precisely as Madame Delphine gradually sells the corner
lots of her property for ready cash (31). Cable underscores the sense of a
neighborhood in socioeconomic decline by speaking of the "architectural
decrepitude" in the area, of the "ancient and foreign-seeming domestic life"
that "over-hangs the ruins of a former commercial prosperity." As is seen in
the opening of " 'Sieur George," Cable is focusing on the deterioration of
buildings to suggest the socioeconomic deterioration of the residents. But
just as important, Cable is blurring the past and the present for dramatic
effect: the picturesque contemporary New Orleans known to tourists is
characterized as "a city of merchants" full of "activity and clatter"; but
literally a stone's throw away, there coexist "the ruins of a *former* commercial
prosperity" (emphasis mine). Cable's point could not be more clear: the
"long sabbath of decay" that has settled upon parts of New Orleans can—
indeed, will—spread to the apparently secure "Americanized" commercial

world surrounding Canal Street. The deterioration of a community as the result of socioeconomic injustice is closer to us—physically, temporally, and, indeed, morally—than we may care to admit; and its effects, far from being confined to a distant, isolated neighborhood, spread like a debilitating disease or blight—a quality powerfully conveyed in the unfortunate ethnic slur about "that significant fungus, the Chinaman." In fine, although William Bedford Clark argues that "the story stops short of portraying the eventual consequences of the white South's racial transgressions,"[6] that grim future is subtly but potently suggested in the juxtaposition of the thriving Canal Street and the dying Rue Royale. The writing is on the wall.

Curiously, the impression of "a squalor almost oriental," which Cable has so carefully created in this second paragraph, is less compromised than heightened by the subsequent discussion of the neighborhood's hidden beauty:

> Yet beauty lingers here. To say nothing of the picturesque, sometimes you get sight of comfort, sometimes of opulence, through the unlatched wicket in some *porte-cochère*—red-painted brick pavement, foliage of dark palm or pale banana, marble or granite masonry and blooming parterres; or through a chink between some pair of heavy batten window-shutters, opened with an almost reptile wariness, your eye gets a glimpse of lace and brocade upholstery, silver and bronze, and much similar rich antiquity.
>
> The faces of the inmates are in keeping; of the passengers in the street a sad proportion are dingy and shabby; but just when these are putting you off your guard, there will pass you a woman—more likely two or three—of patrician beauty. (2)

It is of the utmost importance that the "lace and brocade upholstery, silver and bronze" can only be seen by "a glimpse"; the motif of concealment—including its companion motifs of unclear identities and inappropriate labels—is a typical Cablesque element that assumes particular importance in this story of untruths, secret sin, and past mistakes. The beauty to be found in the neighborhood around the Rue Royale is not readily apparent. That something attractive must be hidden—indeed, locked up behind "heavy batten window-shutters"—indicates the palpable fear of the worsening decay and, concomitantly, the unnaturalness of the situation that decay generates: beauty, like Madame Delphine's love for her daughter, is something to be concealed or denied, rather than acknowledged freely and openly. Moreover, that beauty must be actively sought. Using a technique that anticipates Capitaine Lemaitre's peeking into doors and windows to find Olive, Cable suggests that "you" *can* perceive the hope, the beauty, underlying the sensitive and complex issue of miscegenation—but only if you actively seek it. Finally, that the beauty only "lingers" suggests that time is running out: passivity guarantees dissolution.

That the careful juxtaposition of "patrician beauty" and oriental squalor is intended specifically to refer to the situation of Madame Delphine is evident in Cable's narrowing of his focus from the New Orleans familiar to tourists, to the neighborhood around Rue Royale, to her house:[7]

> Now, if you will go far enough down this old street, you will see, as you approach its intersection with ———. Names in that region elude one like ghosts.
>
> However, as you begin to find the way a trifle more open, you will not fail to notice on the right-hand side, about midway of the square, a small, low, brick house of a story and a half, set out upon the sidewalk, as weather-beaten and mute as an aged beggar fallen asleep. . . . You can almost touch with your cane the low edge of the broad, over-hanging eaves. The batten shutters at door and window, with hinges like those of a postern, are shut with a grip that makes one's knuckles and nails feel lacerated. Save in the brick-work itself there is not a cranny. You would say the house has the lockjaw. . . . Continuing on down the sidewalk, on a line with the house, is a garden masked from view by a high, close board-fence. You may see the tops of its fruit-trees. . . . (2–3)

Using a technique that is characteristic of Cable's writing, the tour-guide narrator does not know the name of the street where Madame Delphine lived so many years before: "Names in that region elude one like ghosts." The reference to ghosts is in keeping with the blurring of the past and present, of romance and harshness, which is the single most striking feature of the story; indeed, one tends to overlook the fact that the bulk of the sad tale is an extended flashback sequence, the events having happened "sixty years ago and more" (4). Further, the reference to ghosts anticipates the death of Madame Delphine at the tale's conclusion, while also suggesting the living death of herself and her daughter—of all quadroons and oc-toroons[8]—as they avoid contact with the white-dominated society. But just as important, the failure to know—or to reveal—the name of the street is a reflection of the concealment and the unclear identities that are a built-in consequence of the injustices of the Code Noir. These qualities are evident in the house of Madame Delphine, with its "batten shutters" closed "with a grip that makes one's knuckles and nails feel lacerated." These details impart a negative quality to the seemingly offhand remark that "You can almost touch with your cane the low edge of the broad, over-hanging eaves"; instead of being the innocent act of a charmed tourist, it seems to be more a threat—yet another instance of a Caucasian male attempting to invade the sanctity of the home of an innocent quadroon and her helpless daughter. Further, Madame Delphine's house seems to have "the lockjaw." In addition to being a manifestation of the disease motif introduced earlier in the story, lockjaw suggests concealment, anger, death (rigor mortis) and, most em-phatically, a refusal to speak—singularly appropriate for a story in which much of what is said is a lie. Likewise, Madame Delphine's garden (which is much like that of the "Café des Exilés") is evidently a beautiful place concealed from the harsh outside world by "a high, close board-fence." Cable is especially careful to call the garden "masked," a clear reference to the quadroon balls where Madame Delphine, presumably wearing the traditional satin mask, danced and became the mistress of the man who fathered Olive.

As Cable begins to conclude his introductory chapter, a neighbor "drops the simple key to the whole matter" to the inquiring tourist: " 'Dey's quadroons' " (3–4). Cable will wait more than seventy pages to explain that "the whole matter" specifically refers to the "close-sealed, uninhabited look" of the house (77), and the delayed explanation proves eloquent: "the whole matter" most insistently refers to the plight of those who live in the house, but it also, by extension, refers to all the ugliness and beauty that have been so carefully rendered for the previous three pages, and, by further extension, to everything that will be elucidated in the subsequent seventy pages. The "simple key" opens, as it were, a Pandora's box of elements that many people, from throughout the United States, would rather leave concealed.

In the last paragraph of the first chapter, Cable finally narrows his focus to Madame Delphine herself:

> Here dwelt, sixty years ago and more, one Delphine Carraze; or, as she was commonly designated by the few who knew her, Madame Delphine. That she owned her home, and that it had been given her by the then deceased companion of her days of beauty, were facts so generally admitted as to be, even as far back as that sixty years ago, no longer a subject of gossip. She was never pointed out by the denizens of the quarter as a character, nor her house as a "feature." It would have passed all Creole powers of guessing to divine what you could find worthy of inquiry concerning a retired quadroon woman; and not the least puzzled of all would have been the timid and restive Madame Delphine herself. (4)

As a manifestation of his love of wordplay and his tendency to allegorize, Cable was much inclined to provide his characters with symbolic names. The given name "Delphine," for example, suggests "delphinium," and thus is consistent with the vegetative imagery of this and the other stories of *Old Creole Days*. It may also have been inspired by Delphine d'Albemar, the heroine of Madame de Staël's 1802 romantic tragedy, *Delphine*. Despite its sentimental tone, this epistolary novel of doomed love makes serious statements about the education of women, freedom of religious conscience, and political equality—issues close to the heart of Cable, and very much evident throughout *Madame Delphine*. For the reader to detect similarities between Cable's story and Madame de Staël's popular novel would serve only to enhance *Madame Delphine,* to convey emphatically that the Rousseauesque ideals that she had presented fictionally some eighty years earlier are also the basis for the seemingly radical notions on racial freedom posited in Cable's novella. The given name "Delphine" was thus chosen with care; and so too was the surname "Carraze." Anyone familiar with Cable's fiction realizes that he presents dialect (either patois or broken English) through phonetic spelling; the word "Carraze," pulled out of context, could readily be interpreted as "Crazy." The ironic appropriateness of this becomes clear in the course of the story, as Cable has every one of the sympathetic characters (Père Jerome, Capitaine Lemaitre, Olive, Madame Delphine) described as "odd," unconventional, abnormal. Lemaitre, for example, fears he is a lunatic (43), and Madame Delphine herself is termed "crazy" by her own daughter (67). As Cable well knew from the shocked South's rejection of his own public espousals of Negro rights,[9] challenges to the situation generated by the Code Noir on the grounds of logic or humanitarianism were seen as evidence of mental imbalance: the irrational had become the norm. A subtle indicator of this phenomenon is seen in the remark that Madame Delphine "was never pointed out by the denizens of the quarter as a character, nor her house as a 'feature'" (4). Cable is making a chilling indictment of New Orleans under the Code Noir by suggesting that for a woman to be a quadroon, to be the mistress of a white man, and to have an illegitimate child are so much a part of quotidian reality, so "normal" by local standards, that they generate no interest whatsoever. Even "the timid and restive Madame Delphine" herself would be surprised that anyone might find her case worthy of notice (4).

The second chapter of Cable's novella is designed to explain how this passive acceptance of a scandalous situation came about. Dropping the stance of tour guide, the narrator assumes a Hawthornesque role of social historian, explaining carefully how the "golden age" of the "free quadroon caste" came into being during "the first quarter of the present century" (4). The moral laxity that Cable tended to associate with Iberian blood (most notably in the character of Mazaro in "Café des Exilés") comes into full play: the ancestors of the quadroons of Madame Delphine's era (the 1820s) were "sprung, upon the one hand, from the merry gallants of a French colonial military service which had *grown gross by affiliation with Spanish-American frontier life,* and, upon the other hand, from comely Ethiopians culled out of the less negroidal types" of blacks (4–5, emphasis mine). The phrase "less negroidal" shows Cable's customary downplaying of the black ancestry of his sympathetic mixed-blood characters, but the passage is particularly important in that the emphasis is on genetics. It cannot be forgotten that the children of these early unions were half French, and in fact the description of the quadroons during the 1820s makes them sound like stereotypical French women:

[A]s the present century was in its second and third decades, the *quad-roones* (for we must contrive a feminine spelling to define the strict limits of the caste as then established) came forth in splendor. Old travellers spare no terms to tell their praises, their faultlessness of feature, their perfection of form, their varied styles of beauty,—for there were even pure Caucasian blondes among them,—their fascinating manners, their sparkling vivacity, their chaste and pretty wit, their grace in the dance, their modest propriety, their taste and elegance in dress. In the gentlest and most poetic sense they were indeed the sirens of this land, where it seemed "always afternoon"—a momentary triumph of an Arcadian over a Christian civilization, so beautiful and so seductive that it became the subject of special chapters by writers of the day more original than correct as social philosophers. (5–6)

It also cannot be forgotten that these "Arcadian" beauties were the products of "seventy-five years devoted to the elimination of the black pigment and the cultivation of hyperian excellence and nymphean grace and beauty" (5). Cable is making several vital points. First, the quadroons are not distinguishable from white women; the phrase "*pure* Caucasian blondes" is, then, an example of Cable's penchant for ironic wordplay. Although it is probably true that Cable is enlisting his audience's sympathy less for the black blood in the quadroons than for the significantly larger portion of white blood, the fact remains that nothing could more graphically suggest the arbitrariness and cruelty of the Code Noir than the simple fact that one cannot identify a quadroon on the basis of physical appearance; one's "race" is solely a matter of birth certificates and documents—a reality that, iron-ically, Madame Delphine is able to use to her advantage by falsely swearing that Olive is not her daughter. A classification system that had been based on genetics had degenerated into a purely legal one—an absurd situation that appalled Kate Chopin ("Désirée's Baby") as much as Cable. Further, even by Caucasian standards, the quadroons were exceptional in appearance and personality. That "old travellers"—people whose age and experience would put them in an ideal position to know—found the quadroons ex-traordinary would further underscore the cruelty of a system that regarded that as personae non gratae, with even fewer civil rights than were enjoyed by the most undesirable members of Caucasian society. Finally, the quad-roons of the 1820s were the products of a system begun at least seventy-five years before, and the unjust world of the frame story of *Madame Delphine* is set more than sixty years later. In effect, Cable is arguing that the discrimi-natory laws of the 1880s were the product of a long-term (more than 130 years) situation. As a result, the problems they generated were "interwoven into the fabric of the community" and thus could not be "facilely extricated and eliminated."[10] Moreover, even though these laws were so firmly estab-lished, they simply were no longer relevant to contemporary conditions:

Madame Delphine's daughter Olive, although " 'seven parts white' " (62), was legally black in the 1820s, and—legally speaking—so would be the descendants of herself and her white husband some sixty years later. The condemnation of the laws of the 1880s is apparent (albeit subtle) in Cable's description of the "Arcadian" quadroons of the 1820s, and it is similarly apparent in his presentation of the quadroon balls. These dances "were got up for them by the male *sang-pur*":

> The magnates of government,—municipal, state, federal,—those of the army, of the learned professions and of the clubs,—in short, the white male aristocracy in every thing save the ecclesiastical desk,—were there. Tickets were high-priced to insure the exclusion of the vulgar. (6)

In effect, the very individuals who conducted the quadroon balls in the first place were responsible for designing and implementing the laws that stripped the civil rights of the children of the sexual liaisons formed at the quadroon balls—in effect, of their own children. But although immediate blame for the unjust situation of the 1880s is laid squarely on the shoulders of "the magnates of government" of the 1820s, one need not read far into the story to realize that Cable extends that blame to anyone in the 1880s— New Orleanian or New Yorker—who passively accepts the situation in the South.

It is significant in this regard that although the quadroon balls were a sexual as well as a racial institution, Cable goes to great lengths to avoid blaming the mixed-blood women themselves for being involved in what was virtually legalized prostitution; in particular, he downplays their sexuality. The quadroons were sirens "in the gentlest and most poetic sense"; their wit was "chaste"; their propriety was "modest"; and while at the balls, there was evident "a pathos in their charm that gave them a family likeness to innocence" (6). Madame Delphine herself had been the mistress of a man she had met at the quadroon balls, but Cable downplays this illicit sexual liaison by speaking of it in terms of a marriage: "her husband—let us call him so for her sake—was long dead"; she is characterized by "a gentle thoughtfulness of expression which would take long to describe: call it a widow's look"; and, as with many widows, her life is greatly curtailed: her "chief occupation and end in life seemed to be to keep well locked up indoors" (6–7). In short, their relationship, although illicit, was closer to the ideal of a good marriage than would be most legal ones. Cable clearly is questioning the validity of legal "identities" (mistress and wife), while simultaneously generating sympathy for Madame Delphine. But he also is subtly implicating the Northern readership. Madame Delphine's husband "was an American, and, if we take her word for it, a man of noble heart and extremely handsome; but this is knowledge which we can do without" (6). In point of fact, his being an American is a bit of information we can not "do without." Cable's seemingly offhand remark suggests that the problem of mixed blood is not a New Orleans issue, or a Louisiana issue, or even a Southern one: it is an American one, and the entire country—by acquiescence if not by overt act—is responsible for racial injustice.

With the third chapter of *Madame Delphine,* Cable introduces a character of considerable promise who proves to be one of the weakest aspects of the novella—Capitaine Ursin Lemaitre-Vignevielle. The initial presentation of Lemaitre suggests that he is a stock character out of sentimental fiction. "He was one of those men that might be of any age,—thirty, forty, forty-five; there was no telling from his face what was years and what was only weather" (7); and, always sensitive to the capacity of description to facilitate characterization, Cable endows him with the most sentimentally appealing features: "His countenance was of a grave and quiet, but also luminous, sort, which was instantly admired and ever afterward remembered, as was also the fineness of his hair and the blueness of his eyes" (7). Lemaitre was an orphan (an endearing detail), and so was cared for by "a rugged old military grandpa of the colonial school," whose idea of raising the child was to remind him perpetually of the fact that " 'none of your family line ever kept the laws of any government or creed' " (8). Any devotee of sentimental fiction can imagine what will become of him: he will fall in with Bad Company (the piratical brothers Lafitte, no less), but he will be saved by the love and faith of a Good Woman (Olive, of course). True, Cable does try to salvage Lemaitre from the dubious level of sentimental hero by rendering his character somewhat unique (he is "odd," and has an unlikely passion for bookkeeping [7, 9]), but the fact remains that he never quite materializes; and during the remarkably long stretches when he is absent from the novella he is not missed in the least. But chapter 3 is nevertheless vital for the further development of the motifs and techniques presented in the first two chapters, as well as for the introduction of several new ones. First, Cable is emphatic that Lemaitre was raised to break laws; as shall be seen, the most positive acts in the story invariably involve the deliberate breaking of laws or the defiance of social convention by ostensibly "crazy" people. Further, although the references to the Lafitte brothers are a reflection of Cable's personal interest in New Orleans history and a concession to the vogue for historical romance that was sweeping the country, they also facilitate the presentation of the unclear identities motif (people will tend to confuse Lemaitre and the Lafittes), as well as of the inappropriate labels motif. Much as Madame Delphine could be labeled either as mistress or wife, and her daughter as white or black (depending upon the legal documents at hand), the brothers Lafitte—and, consequently, their associate Lemaitre—receive various labels: "Smuggler—patriot—where was the difference?" (9). After a while, "smuggling began to lose its respectability"; "the business became unprofitable for a time until the enterprising Lafittes—thinkers—bethought them of a corrective—'privateering' " (10). And after they refused "money and rank" to fight on the side of Britain in the War of 1812, "their heads were ruled out of the market, and, meeting and treating with Andrew Jackson, they were received as lovers of their country" (10–11). That public opinion alone could so modify the social status of common criminals holds out significant possibilities for the modification of the status of quadroons through solid public relations work; and Cable, whose desire for social reform ostensibly compromised his artistic sense in his later career,[11] would have been well aware of the potential of his novella as an instrument of reform. Finally, Cable offers yet another seemingly offhand but significant detail: Lemaitre's grandfather tried to raise him to be "as savage and ferocious a holder of unimpeachable social rank as it became a pure-blooded French Creole to be who would trace his pedigree back to the god Mars" (8). Even if we make allowance for grandfatherly jesting, the suggestion that anyone could trace his ancestry back to a mythological being indicates the absurdity of the whole concept of "pure-bloodedness." Despite his superficially impressive, hyphenated surname ("Lemaitre" is translatable as "the master"; "Vignevielle" means "old vine," as in "vintage grape vine"), and despite his aristocratic upbringing and romantic career as a pirate, Ursin is essentially just another Frenchman whose ancestry may be even more doubtful or "tainted" than Olive's. In the long run it would have been to Cable's advantage to develop further the character of Lemaitre, to qualify the strong impression of him as the blue-blooded pirate with the heart of gold. But to do so might blur the focus upon Madame Delphine and Olive, and it would necessitate a broader canvas on which to work. If *Madame Delphine* occasionally seems less like a novella than a truncated or abortive novel, much of the blame must rest on Cable's decision not to develop the possibilities inherent in the character of Capitaine Lemaitre.

The same problem is evident in Cable's presentation of the "Three Friends" of chapter 4. By virtue of longtime friendship or marriage, each of the three men (Père Jerome, Evariste Varrillat, and Jean Thompson) is involved in the personal life of Lemaitre—including, of course, his desire to enter into an illegal marriage with Olive, an octoroon. It would appear that each of the three men was intended to explore the problem of miscegenation from the approach peculiar to his temperament: as a priest, Père Jerome would use the spiritual approach; Evariste Varrillat, a physician, would use the genetic approach first hinted at in the second chapter; and Jean Thompson, an attorney, would use the legal approach. With each man voicing the position of his particular field of expertise, *Madame Delphine* would serve as a forum through which Cable could present the prevailing beliefs and attitudes toward mixed blood held by a broad cross section of society; further, with the three positions being played off, each against the others, the flaws and strengths of each would be thrown into relief, and perhaps some sort of mutually acceptable resolution could be achieved. It is an ambitious scheme—too ambitious, in fact, for a novella. Of the three men, only Père Jerome commands attention for any length of time. Varrillat is scarcely noticeable in the story, a particularly unfortunate situation since the questions he poses in chapter 4 do force Père Jerome to clarify his position on spiritual matters. Further, he accurately diagnoses the fact that it was love, not faith, that compelled Lemaitre not to plunder the ship carrying Olive to New Orleans: " ' . . . I tell you w'ad is sure-sure! Ursin Lemaitre din kyare nut'n fo' doze creed; *he fall in love!* ' " (16, Cable's emphasis). The lawyer Jean Thompson is presented in chapter 4 as obstinate and aggressive, a sort of legal hairsplitter who insists that his childhood playmate Lemaitre is not engaged in any illegal activities: " 'He is no pirate; he has merely taken out letters of marque and reprisal under the flag of the republic of Carthagena' " (14). Significantly, neither the theoretically objective and observant physician, nor the obstinate and defensive attorney, will accept the truths presented by the spiritual leader, Père Jerome:

> "There was on the ship a young girl [Olive] who was very beautiful. She came on deck, where the corsair stood, about to issue his orders, and, more beautiful than ever in the desperation of the moment, confronted him with a small missal spread open, and, her finger on the Apostles' Creed, commanded him to read. He read it, uncovering his head as he read, then stood gazing on her face, which did not quail; and then with a low bow, said: 'Give me this book and I will do your bidding.' She gave him the book and bade him leave the ship, and he left it unmolested."
>
> Père Jerome looked from the physician to the attorney and back again, once or twice, with his dimpled smile.
>
> "But he speaks English, they say," said Jean Thompson.
>
> "He has, no doubt, learned it since he left us," said the priest.
>
> "But this ship-master, too, says his men called him Lafitte."
>
> "Lafitte? No. Do you not see? It is your brother-in-law, Jean Thompson! It is your wife's brother! Not Lafitte, but" (softly) "Lemaitre! Lemaitre! Capitaine Ursin Lemaitre!"
>
> The two guests looked at each other with a growing drollery on either face, and presently broke into a laugh. (15–16)

As is evident from most of the other stories of *Old Creole Days* (all of which predate *Madame Delphine*), Cable had a strong tendency to use a religious approach to explore major personal and social ills. It is to his credit that in *Madame Delphine* he did at least acknowledge the existence of other approaches, but by not developing them adequately he left the novella oddly unbalanced. For all intents and purposes, Varrillat and Thompson are scarcely evident for some fifty pages after they are introduced. That they later are rumored to harbor the fugitive ex-pirate (65) seems more the act of friends and relatives than of the two spokesmen for genetics and law. Cable simply does not take advantage of the possibilities of the situation. And when the two men finally do emerge and speak in the story—fully ten chapters (out of fifteen) after their initial appearance—the reader sees but a glimmer of the drama inherent in a situation wherein friendship, kinship, love, genetics, and law are all at odds. It is a serious thematic and technical problem to which we shall return shortly.

The character of Père Jerome, however, is far more successful than that of Capitaine Lemaitre, Varrillat, or Thompson. Cable himself perceived him as serving essentially the same purpose as Joseph Frowenfeld of *The Grandissimes,* but felt that Père Jerome was a finer artistic achievement. As Cable wrote to William Dean Howells in 1881,

> Alas! Poor Frowenfeld; I knew I should never raise that child. The goody-goody die young. But—speaking in earnest—it was my chagrin over my partial failure with him that determined me to write out a character who should be pious and yet satisfactory to the artistic sense; hence Père Jerome in the story of Madame Delphine.[12]

Cable's determination not to make Père Jerome a "goody-goody" is evident in the details he provides. Although "one could smell distinctly . . . the vow of poverty" throughout his home, one could also smell odors "of a more epicurean sort, that explained interestingly the Père Jerome's rotundity and rosy smile" (12). He also can not—or will not—prevent Madame Delphine from lying about her daughter's parentage (69); he is human enough to perspire—from humidity and stress—while in the confessional (77–78); and he chastises himself for feeling too "saintly" in the Cathedral:

> "Be not deceived, Père Jerome, because saintliness of feeling is easy here; you are the same priest who overslept this morning, and over-ate yesterday, and will, in some way, easily go wrong to-morrow and the day after." (19)

But the two features of Père Jerome that most effectively prevent him from becoming another Frowenfeld are that he is a native New Orleanian and personally unconventional. Cable is quite explicit that "He was a Creole and a member of one of the city's leading families" (11). For a prominent native of New Orleans to question the Code Noir—let alone knowingly perform the wedding of a Caucasian and an octoroon—adds considerable impact to Cable's story. It is not a situation in which an ignorant outsider (like the German-American Frowenfeld) tries to change a complex, alien social system, but rather one in which the challenge comes from someone who is painfully familiar with the system and whose family has surely supported—and probably even benefited from—it. As Louis D. Rubin, Jr. writes, Père Jerome "might be said to represent Cable's attempt to disarm those who accused him of denigrating Creole morality, by letting the critique of racism come this time from a Creole priest with no Anglo-Americans on the scene to prompt him."[13] The insistently New Orleanian background of Père Jerome is thus part and parcel with Cable's remarks that Olive's father was an American (6), and that the lawyer Jean Thompson is "half Américain" (13). No one group—Creole or American—is pure villainy or pure innocence. And the social criticism implicit in Père Jerome's stance is not qualified by the fact that by nature he is an iconoclast. He writes regularly to the pirate Lemaitre (17), and is something of a renegade priest: "among the clergy there were two or three who shook their heads and raised their eyebrows, and said he would be at least as orthodox if he did not make quite so much of the Bible and quite so little of the dogmas" (17). His defiant support of the socially unacceptable romance of Lemaitre and Olive, even to the point of sending them to France "where the law offered no obstacles" (65), suggests that Père Jerome is literary kin to Friar Laurence, the humanly frail helpmate of Romeo and Juliet who hoped to guide them to wedded bliss in Mantua. The fullness and humanity of Père Jerome's characterization incline the reader to accept what he says about the " 'community of responsibility attaching to every misdeed' " (13), and they also help generate the concern (albeit limited) we feel about the love affair between Lemaitre and Olive.

The concept of the "community of responsibility" is first presented in the course of the discussion between Père Jerome, Varrillat, and Thompson in chapter 4. Père Jerome defends their friend Lemaitre's career as a pirate on these grounds:

> "It is impossible for any finite mind to fix the degree of criminality of any human act or of any human life. The Infinite One alone can know how much of our sin is chargeable to us, and how much to our brothers or our fathers. We all participate in one another's sins. There is a community of responsibility attaching to every misdeed. No human since Adam—nay, nor Adam himself—ever sinned entirely to himself. And so I never am called upon to contemplate a crime or a criminal but I feel my conscience pointing at me as one of the accessories." (13)

The concept that we all (either by act or acquiescence) are personally responsible for an individual's mistakes is reiterated in chapter 5, "The Cap Fits," most of which reconstructs Père Jerome's 1821 Christmas sermon on St. Stephen:

> "Notice these, the tenderest words of the tenderest prayer that ever came from the lips of a blessed martyr—the dying words of the holy Saint Stephen, 'Lord, lay not this sin to their charge.' Is there nothing dreadful in that? Read it thus: 'Lord, lay not this sin to *their* charge.' Not to the charge of them who stoned him? To whose charge then? Go ask the holy

Saint Paul. Three years afterward . . . he answered that question: 'I stood by and consented.' He answered for himself only; but the Day must come when all that wicked council that sent Saint Stephen away to be stoned, and all that city of Jerusalem, must hold up the hand and say: 'We, also, Lord—we stood by.' Ah! friends, under the simpler meaning of that dying saint's prayer for the pardon of his murderers is hidden the terrible truth that we all have a share in one another's sins."

Thus Père Jerome touched his key-note. All that time has spared us beside may be given in a few sentences.

"Ah!" he cried once, "if it were merely my own sins that I had to answer for, I might hold up my head before the rest of mankind; but no, no, my friends—we cannot look each other in the face, for each has helped the other to sin. Oh, where is there any room, in this world of common disgrace, for pride? Even if we had no common hope, a common despair ought to bind us together and forever silence the voice of scorn!" (19–20, Cable's emphasis)

Père Jerome specifically applies this belief to the situation of Lemaitre, whose career as a pirate is overtly blamed on the congregation ("'you, monsieur, and you, madame, sitting here in your *smuggled clothes*'" [22–23, Cable's emphasis]). But Cable also makes it clear that Père Jerome is speaking of the Code Noir. After the priest "with a stir of deep pity" notices Madame Delphine and Olive in the congregation (20), he states that "'there are thousands of people in this city of New Orleans to whom society gives the ten commandments of God with all the *nots* rubbed out! . . . if God sends the poor weakling to purgatory for leaving the right path, where ought some of you to go who strew it with thorns and briers!'" (21) Interestingly, Cable drives home the theme of the community of responsibility not only by repeating it throughout the story, but also by grounding it in a rather surprising metaphor: the celestial account book.[14] The novella features a remarkable number of references to accounts and charges, including the incrementally repeated "Lord, lay not this sin to [his, her, their] charge"; and the special theological significance of these references becomes clear in the course of Père Jerome's sermon. The priest reveals that Lemaitre, while pirating, suddenly found himself "thrown into the solemn companionship with the sea, with the air, with the storm, the calm, the heavens by day, the heavens by night" (22). As a variation on the traditional idea that Nature is the Great Book of God, Cable—himself the former bookkeeper for William C. Black & Co., cotton factors—argues that Lemaitre comes to perceive God as a sort of Heavenly Bookkeeper: "[O]ne night there came to him, like a spirit walking on the sea, the awful, silent question: 'My account with God—how does it stand?'" (22). As Cable develops this motif, it becomes clear that no one individual is ever solely "charged" for his personal transgressions, and this, in turn, helps place into proper perspective the past mistakes of Madame Delphine (living in sin, having a child out of wedlock): " 'She is a quadroone; all the rights of her womanhood trampled in the mire, sin made easy to her—almost compulsory,—charge it to account of whom it may concern' " (26). Even the one "sin" we watch her commit—testifying falsely that Olive is not her daughter (chapter 14)—is not truly her fault: " 'Lord, lay not this sin to her charge!' " (81) And lest the reader conclude that Père Jerome is speaking only of the sinful community of New Orleans, Cable is careful to implicate the entire country. As Père Jerome bluntly observes, where a quadroon is concerned, " 'every white man *in this country,* on land or on water, is a pirate' " (29, emphasis mine).

The theme of the community of responsibility is at the heart of *Madame Delphine*. It is this ethical dimension, argued William M. Baskervill in 1897, that prevents the story from being "a fairy tale for quadroons."[15] But the "fairy tale" element is nonetheless present, and it is most obvious in the relationship between Lemaitre and Olive. As was noted earlier, Lamaitre barely materializes. He is a sentimental hero whose postpiracy career as a philanthropic banker (he admittedly runs his bank as " 'a charitable institution' " [39] merely compounds his incredible characterization as a sort of Robin Hood of Crescent City. The story of his initial meeting with Olive— first told by Père Jerome privately to his friends, and then worked into his sermon—is, as Rubin notes, "the kind of romantic plot so popular at the time."[16] Having been rescued from a life of crime by a fair damsel with a prayer book, Lemaitre assumes a new identity ("It was Capitaine Lemaitre who had disappeared; it was Monsieur Vignevielle who had come back" [38]), and, nattily attired in blue cottonade and white duck shoes (29, 30, 32), he searches for the girl whose "face and form" had "turned him face about from the way of destruction" (41). For all intents and purposes, Lemaitre is an example of the benevolent voyeur who figures so prominently in *Old Creole Days*; but he lacks the fundamental nobility inherent in the other voyeurs simply because Cable tries so desperately to make him special. All of the gushings of Père Jerome (" 'He is God's own banker' " [31] and all of the narrator's avowals of his charmed life ("He was one of those men for whom danger appears to stand aside" [40]) only render all the more ludicrous the idea of a bookkeeper-turned-pirate-turned-banker who roams New Orleans at night in search of his female savior. It would have been good satire if Cable had known it was satire. The ludicrousness of Cable's characterization of the spoony ex-pirate is even more apparent when one considers the characterization of Olive.

Cable apparently sought to make Olive an individualized, appealing character; but, curiously, she is more interesting when we are given information about her than when she herself speaks or acts. That her ancestors were French gallants and comely Ethiopians (chapter 2) and that, missal in hand, she reportedly stood up to a pirate, are pieces of information that predispose the reader to find her attractive and admirable even before she first appears in the story. That first appearance occurs, significantly, in the Cathedral, where "scrupulously concealed" by a heavy veil and gloves, the devout Olive listens to Père Jerome tell of her dramatic meeting with the pirate Lemaitre (20). Olive will not figure prominently in the story until her near-encounter with Lemaitre in the garden some twenty pages later—that is, approximately halfway through the novella. In the lengthy interim we learn that she was raised by her American father's mother and sisters (27), that she is "sweet" and "good" (38), and that " 'you would never believe she was [Madame Delphine's] daughter; she is white and beautiful' " (27). To nineteenth-century readers, Olive would qualify as a sterling example of what Jules Zanger identified in 1966 as "the tragic octoroon":

> Briefly summarized, the "tragic octoroon" is a beautiful young girl who possesses only the slightest evidences of Negro blood, who speaks with no trace of dialect, who was raised and educated as a white child and as a lady in the household of her father, and who on her paternal side is descended from "some of the best blood in the 'Old Dominion.' " In her sensibility and her vulnerability she resembles, of course, the conventional ingenue "victim" of sentimental romance. Her condition is radically changed when, at her father's unexpected death, it is revealed that he has failed to free her properly. She discovers that she is a slave;
> . . .[17]

Although Zanger is referring specifically to antebellum fictional octoroons, and although certain details must be modified (Olive left her father's hometown when "The sisters married, the mother died" [27], and technically she is "free"), the fact remains that Olive is essentially a stock figure out of a particular type of nineteenth-century popular romance; and Cable is as unable to breathe life into her as he is into her equally wooden lover. The basic problems with Olive—and concomitantly, with the love affair that is meant to serve as the dramatic center of the novella—are readily apparent in the garden scene. Persisting in his nightly quest for the unknown girl who turned him away from piracy, Lemaitre-Vignevielle is attracted by a mockingbird to a garden redolent with "the overpowering sweetness of the night-jasmine" (41). The bulk of the scene deserves to be quoted:

> He stepped in and drew the gate to after him. There, very near by, was the clump of jasmine, whose ravishing odor had tempted him. It stood just beyond a brightly moonlit path, which turned from him in a curve toward the residence . . . While he still looked, there fell upon his ear, from around that curve, a light footstep on the broken shells—one only, and then all was for a moment still again. Had he mistaken? No. The same soft click was repeated nearer by, a pale glimpse of robes came through the tangle, and then, plainly to view, appeared an outline—a presence—a form—a spirit—a girl!

From throat to instep she was as white as Cynthia. Something above the medium height, slender, lithe, her abundant hair rolling in dark, rich waves back from her brows and down from her crown, and falling in two heavy plaits beyond her round, broadly girt waist and full to her knees, a few escaping locks eddying lightly on her graceful neck and her temples,—her arms, half hid in a snowy mist of sleeve, let down to guide her spotless skirts free from the dewy touch of the grass,—straight down the path she came!

Will she stop? Will she turn aside? Will she espy the dark form in the deep shade of the orange, and, with one piercing scream, wheel and vanish? She draws near. She approaches the jasmine; she raises her arms, the sleeves falling like a vapor down to the shoulders; . . . O Memory! Can it be? *Can it be?* Is this his quest, or is it lunacy? The ground seems to Monsieur Vignevielle the unsteady sea, and he to stand once more on a deck. And she? As she is now, if she but turn toward the orange, the whole glory of the moon will shine upon her face. His heart stands still; . . . That neck and throat! . . . Now she fastens a spray in her hair. The mocking-bird cannot withhold; he breaks into song—she turns—she turns her face—it is she, it is she! Madame Delphine's daughter is the girl he met on the ship. (42–43, Cable's emphasis)

Like the sentimental tales out of which the characters of Lemaitre and Olive were drawn,[18] the passage is embarrassingly overwritten. Cable's determination to underscore the sweetness and innocence of Olive by associating her with jasmine and mockingbirds[19] is well meant but overdone. Even more strident is her association with the moon, although this is perhaps defensible on the grounds of complexity. First, the moon (more precisely, Diana) is the protectoress of chastity. As noted earlier, Cable goes to great lengths to downplay the unfortunate sexual implications of labels such as "quadroon" or "octoroon," and in this garden scene the sensuous diction is reserved for the jasmine ("ravishing," "tempted") rather than the girl. Second, the moon is white. For Olive to be "as white as Cynthia" is a clear reference to the discrepancy between her Caucasian appearance and her black legal status. Third, the moon is associated with insanity: "Is this his quest, or is it lunacy?" Quite appropriate for a society that labels some white people as blacks, and that forces helpless women to deny their maternity so as to ensure their daughters' happiness, the only right-thinking and right-acting people in this story are identified as mentally unbalanced. As Olive will later say of her own mother, " ' . . . *she is* crazy,—and I am no better' " (67, Cable's emphasis). For Lemaitre to meet Olive in the moonlight is, then, a strikingly positive sign. The garden scene also is significant in that it suggests Olive's symbolic function in the story. The word "olive" is a conventional adjective for the complexion of a southern European; hence her given name emphasizes her Caucasian appearance. But the olive is also a traditional symbol of peace and hope, and Olive's status as the repository of positive abstractions dear to Americans is further emphasized by her attire.

Between those locks of hair "eddying lightly on her graceful neck and her temples" and her snowy "chaste drapery" of the "revived classic order" (45), Olive bears a striking resemblance to two ideals traditionally personified as females: liberty and justice. Cable's point is clear: Do we trample peace, hope, liberty, and justice? Or do we permit them to flourish? Our concern over the fate of the relationship between Lemaitre and Olive is, then, meant to be—on a symbolic level—a matter of national import. But this element is significantly compromised simply because it is so difficult to become genuinely interested in two stock characters whose relationship is handled so unconvincingly.

In part, what renders it so unconvincing (aside from the obvious problems with the characterizations of the two lovers) is that we see so little of it. We are told that Lemaitre and Olive first met on a ship, and they almost meet again in the garden scene, which Edmund Gosse—unfortunately without irony—termed "the gem of the book."[20] We know that Lemaitre devotes half of the story to searching for Olive at night, and that Olive pines for the unidentified pirate (48). They finally meet face-to-face in a nicely handled scene in chapter 11, in which the gradually brightening lamp in Madame Delphine's parlor ultimately reveals Lemaitre to Olive (57). The next thing we know, it is three weeks later, and the young people are engaged (58). By providing so little tangible information about the relationship, and by telling us about it more than showing it, Cable is trying to underscore its symbolic aspects. Olive represents any individual of mixed blood, as well as the abstractions indicated previously; and Robert O. Stephens offers a convincing argument that Lemaitre, "Like the pre-war South, . . . is the product of generations of pride and defiance, but after his period of rebellion against Yankee laws he has figuratively died and returned as a new man."[21] The merger of these two symbolic individuals, then, would be quite auspicious. But because the two lovers are not believable as characters, and because their love seems essentially to be a matter of unconvincing hearsay, Cable has, ironically, sacrificed their symbolic impact. We tend not to care for them as people or symbols.

What little we do feel is attributable to the heartfelt concern of Père Jerome and Madame Delphine. His desire to have the young people married, even if it means their moving to France, is palpable. Likewise poignant are Madame Delphine's love for her daughter and guilt over her past transgressions. In many respects, she speaks for Cable. It is she who articulates what everyone feels about the Code Noir: " 'Dad *law* is crezzie! Dad law is a fool!' " (61, Cable's emphasis) In response to Père Jerome's diplomatic attempt to convince her that the law was designed " 'to keep the two races separate,' " Madame Delphine "startled the speaker with a loud, harsh, angry laugh. Fire came from her eyes and her lip curled with scorn":

"Then they made a lie, Père Jerome! Separate! No-o-o! They do not want to keep us separated; no, no! But they *do* want to keep us despised! . . . [F]rom which race do they want to keep my daughter separate? She is seven parts white! The law did not stop her from being that; and now, when she wants to be a white man's good and honest wife, shall that law stop her? Oh, no! . . . I will tell you what that law is made for. It is made to—punish—my—child—for—not—choosing—her—father! Père Jerome—my God, what a law!" (62, Cable's emphasis)

Not surprisingly, it is this "milatraise" (71) who facilitates the resolution of the dilemma by perjuring herself—not, significantly, to any of the people directly involved in the proposed marriage, but to Evariste Varrillat and Jean Thompson. As Lemaitre's kith and kin, Varrillat and Thompson would be expected to support whatever would bring him happiness; but as upstanding members of the white society that supports the Code Noir, they defy their natural inclinations—even to the point of threatening to turn Lemaitre over to the authorities as a former pirate (67). The encounter between Madame Delphine and the doctor and lawyer occurs in the fourteenth chapter, "By an Oath." Thematically and dramatically, it is arguably the most significant chapter in the novella.

As the chapter opens, Père Jerome encounters the distraught Madame Delphine and agrees to conduct her to the house of attorney Jean Thompson. Unable to "withstand her look of entreaty," Père Jerome does not ask how exactly she will " 'put an end to all this trouble' " (69), and in fact he is not present for the climactic scene. Cable begins that scene with a description of the houses of the physician and attorney:

Jean Thompson and Doctor Varrillat lived opposite each other on the Bayou road, a little way beyond the town limits as then prescribed. Each had his large, white-columned, four-sided house among the magnolias,—his huge live-oak overshadowing either corner of the darkly shaded garden, his broad, brick walk leading down to the tall, brick-pillared gate, his square of bright, red pavement on the turf-covered sidewalk, and his railed platform spanning the draining-ditch, with a pair of green benches, one on each edge, facing each other crosswise of the gutter. There, any sunset hour, you were sure to find the householder sitting beside his cool-robed matron, two or three slave nurses in white turbans standing at hand, and an excited throng of fair children, nearly all of a size. (69–70)

Their splendid houses are virtual mirror images of each other. The parallelism tends to compound the magnificence of their material wealth and high social status; in contrast, the tiny, isolated cottage of Madame Delphine suggests her lack of security and status. Further, the parallelism suggests that the two men—and, more broadly, the two orientations they embody (genetic and legal)—are mutually supportive: for either one to question the Code Noir would jeopardize not only his own position, but also that of his associate. Moreover, that the two houses face one another suggests that Madame Delphine will run a symbolic gauntlet as she enters the space between the houses to try to convince the two men that she is not Olive's mother. The stress of that ordeal is by no means mitigated by the domestic bliss of the scene. Those "two or three slave nurses in white turbans" are, in the minds of the Caucasians, accepting a submissive role that Madame Delphine defies. Cable emphasizes that she wears a bonnet and carries a parasol "instead of the turban of her caste" (31), and Jean Thompson is seen "frowning at her law-defying bonnet" (73) as she begins to speak in chapter 14. The scene also stresses the large number of children, and the fact that the "cool-robed" mothers of those children are strongly supportive of—indeed, partly control—their husbands. Jean Thompson cannot even make a joke without looking "at his wife, whose applause he prized" (71), a detail suggesting that the climactic scene takes place at the two men's private homes—rather than at their professional offices—in part to emphasize that they act on behalf of less visible members of society. Further, Cable's details render Madame Delphine's situation acutely painful: as a poor widow, she lacks any sort of emotional support group—spouse, neighbors, servants—even remotely comparable to the veritable psychological and socioeconomic fortress surrounding the Varrillats and Thompsons. Aside from Père Jerome (who, ironically, can only swear to her truthfulness [73] and serve as her confessor) and the ineffectual Lemaitre, Madame Delphine's only viable associate in the novella is her beloved daughter Olive, whom she must publicly reject for the sake of the marriage. One might have expected that the bond of motherhood that Madame Delphine shares with Mesdames Varrillat and Thompson would render them sympathetic to the idea of her denying her only child (biological or adoptive), but even they so benefit from the Code Noir—turbaned slaves raise their children—that they cannot, or will not, feel anything for the plight of Madame Delphine. Indeed, so unfeeling is Madame Thompson that she tells the newly arrived Olive of her mother's disavowal of maternity just moments after Madame Delphine, "turning to the ladies," begged them never to reveal the denial to Olive because " 'It will break her heart'; " (75). The denial itself is handled with striking skill:

> "C'est drole"—it's funny—said Madame Delphine, with a piteous effort to smile, "that nobody thought of it. It is so plain. You have only to look and see. I mean about Olive." She loosed a button in the front of her dress and passed her hand into her bosom. "And yet, Olive herself never thought of it. She does not know a word."

The hand came out holding a miniature. Madame Varrillat passed it to Jean Thompson.

"*Ouala so papa,*" said Madame Delphine. "That is her father."

It went from one to another, exciting admiration and murmured praise.

"She is the image of him," said Madame Thompson, in an austere undertone, returning it to her husband.

Doctor Varrillat was watching Madame Delphine. She was very pale. She had passed a trembling hand into a pocket of her skirt, and now drew out another picture . . . He reached for it, and she handed it to him. He looked at it a moment, when his eyes suddenly lighted up, and he passed it to the attorney.

"*Et là*"—Madame Delphine's utterance failed—"*et là ouala sa moman.* That is her mother."

The three others instantly gathered around Jean Thompson's chair. They were much impressed.

"It is true beyond a doubt!" muttered Madame Thompson.

Madame Varrillat looked at her with astonishment.

"The proof is right there in the faces," said Madame Thompson.

"Yes! yes!" said Madame Delphine, excitedly; "the proof is there! You do not want any better! I am willing to swear to it! But you want no better proof! That is all anybody could want! My God! you cannot help but see it!"

Her manner was wild.

Jean Thompson looked at her sternly.

"Nevertheless you say you are willing to take your solemn oath to this."

"Certainly"—

"You will have to do it."

"Certainly, Miché Thompson, *of course* I shall; you will make out the paper and I will swear before God that it is true! . . ." (74–75, Cable's emphasis)

The miniature of her late husband is kept next to her heart; indeed, Cable's diction (she "passed her hand into her bosom") suggests that the picture *is* her heart. That she must remove something so private and precious and display it to hostile eyes indicates the anguish and desperation she must be experiencing. Further, the act of unbuttoning her dress is suggestive of breast-feeding. Unlike Mesdames Varrillat and Thompson with their slave nurses, Madame Delphine knows what it is like to suckle a child, and the denial of her maternity is thereby rendered all the more poignant. In contrast, the miniature of her husband's half sister is kept in her skirt pocket, a much less emotionally charged location and, symbolically, further from the truth. The reactions to the two miniatures are remarkably ambiguous. When Madame Thompson comments "'It is true beyond a doubt,'" Madame Varrillat "looked at her with astonishment." To what does "her" refer? If it means "the miniature of Olive's mother," then the doctor's wife either believes Madame Delphine's story ("astonishment" equals "an epiph-

any") *or* she cannot comprehend how anyone could lie so transparently
("astonishment" equals "shocked disbelief"). The same contradictory inter-
pretations would apply if "her" referred to Madame Delphine. And if "her"
refers to Madame Thompson, then the doctor's wife does not believe the
story. The same ambiguity is seen with Doctor Varrillat. Although, as a
science-oriented person, he studies Madame Delphine carefully (even going
so far as to note accurately that she walks " 'like a woman in a state of high
nervous excitement' " [71]), his only reaction to the miniature is unclear:
"his eyes suddenly lighted up." Does this mean that he suddenly saw the
"truth" that the woman in the miniature must be Olive's mother? or the
truth that Madame Delphine was perjuring herself? Even Jean Thompson's
reaction is ambiguous. In looking at her "sternly," is he revealing his
attorney's awareness of the body language of a perjurer ("Her manner was
wild") and thereby questioning the truth of what she says? or is he simply
wondering if the solemn oath of a hysterical woman will hold up in court—
regardless of whether what she swears is true? Thanks to Cable's brilliant
use of ambiguity, we do not know whether any of these people genuinely
believes Madame Delphine's story; but we do know they are quite willing to
accept it *if* she will swear to it. As happens so often in Cable's stories, the
truth is inconsequential. Sworn legal documents are all that matter. The
federal agents are perfectly willing to cease their search for Lemaitre because
of their official report "that (to the best of their knowledge and belief, based
on evidence, and especially on the assurances of an unexceptionable eye-
witness, to wit, Monsieur Vignevielle, banker) Capitaine Lemaitre was dead
and buried" (78); and Jean Thompson, "with the affidavit of Madame
Delphine showing through his tightly buttoned coat" (78–79), is more than
happy to witness Olive's wedding to Lemaitre. The truth emerges only in
the confessional; and if it seems a bit melodramatic that Madame Delphine
literally drops dead after confessing her perjury to Père Jerome, the fact
remains that Cable is making a grim appraisal of the status of the truth in
our society: to tell it may be fatal.

If Père Jerome's final words—" 'Lord, lay not this sin to her charge!' "
(81)—sound rather tinny, there is ample reason. It is difficult to believe that
any one would truly consider blaming Madame Delphine for her "sin"; but
more importantly, after eighty pages his dictum has worn quite thin.
Consider the scene between the priest and Madame Delphine as they walk
to the Varrillat and Thompson houses:

It was in the old strain:

"Blame them one part, Madame Delphine, and their fathers, mothers,
brothers, and fellow-citizens the other ninety-nine."

But to every thing she had the one amiable answer which Père Jerome
ignored:

"I am going to arrange it to satisfy everybody, all together. *Tout à fait.*"
(72)

The "old strain" about the community of responsibility has been reiterated so often in the story that it has lost its impact. Robert Underwood Johnson's 1881 appraisal could not be less accurate in describing *Madame Delphine* as

> a readable and picturesque setting of a naturally acted drama on the theme of the inductive or vicarious responsibility for sin. Mr. Cable does not assume the burden of this theme to be proved as a proposition—he is too true an artist for that—but has left it where it ought to rest—upon the characters, and has subdued it to a distinct undertone of a story which owes its main interest to characterization and action. The moral is lightly carried, and not heavily dragged by the movement of the plot: . . . [22]

The theme in fact is far too insistent to be termed an "undertone," and the characters do not—can not—carry the ethical dimension of the story. As has been argued, Lemaitre is a wooden character, rarely present in the novella; Olive is a symbol of abstractions, not a living woman for whom we can care; Madame Delphine is what Rubin terms "too much the conventional helpless mother";[23] the ineffectual Varrillat and the hypocritical Thompson are shadows of the strong characters they might have been; and even Père Jerome seems after a while to be some sort of parrot. As the passage quoted above indicates, even the devout Madame Delphine no longer listens to his often-repeated theory of the community of responsibility because it does not solve her immediate problem—how to marry Olive to Lemaitre. Religious doctrines and practical realities are at odds with one another in *Madame Delphine,* and that is the source of the novella's major conceptual problem: the relationship between Olive and Lemaitre—instead of enriching, illuminating, and testing the story's ethical dimension—seems merely to coexist with it. Curiously, the separate-but-equal status of the story's two centers of interest was especially praised in Cable's day. For example, an anonymous reviewer in the *Nation* (1881) was pleased to find that "its interest as a romance does not at all depend upon its tractarian character."[24] In fact, the "tractarian character" of the story seems to have been of little interest to Cable's contemporary reviewers. Predictably, New Orleans readers took offense at the racial implications of the novella. As Philip Butcher states the case, " . . . Cable kicked up a hornet's nest—or kept the hornets buzzing that he had stirred up about a year earlier with *The Grandissimes,"* for *Madame Delphine* "had very damaging implications for the present": "How many of these Olives, by one deception or another, had brought their taint of Negro blood—imperceptible but legally damning—into some aristocratic Creole family?"[25] Readers outside of New Orleans tended to overlook racial and ethical matters in favor of more tangible ones, such as the dialect. An anonymous 1881 reviewer in *Literary World* found the dialect marvelous:

> . . . a close enunciation of the words as spelled will be found to bring out the dialect with wonderful precision, and to set the mongrel-blooded speakers before the imagination with almost the reality of life. In this, it seems to us, is Mr. Cable's strong point, though we should be sorry to be understood as limiting his powers to a mere repetition of strange talk.[26]

However, many contemporary commentators, including Lafcadio Hearn, found the dialect tiresome,[27] and an anonymous reviewer in the *Nation* took Cable to task for "the apologetic makeshifts resorted to to compass the natural introduction of the dialect."[28] Indeed, Cable's rendering of the dialect is remarkably self-conscious, including such parenthetical explanations as "Both here and elsewhere, let it be understood that where good English is given the words were spoken in good French" (37). But on a more general level, most reviewers seemed content to compare *Madame Delphine*—usually quite favorably—with *The Grandissimes,* which had been published approximately a year before. An anonymous reviewer in *The Critic* (1881) noted that Cable in *Madame Delphine* had shown a "firmer hold of his art" than was evident in the novel; William M. Baskervill termed it "the most perfect specimen of the author's literary art and constructive ability"; and Edmund Gosse declared that *Madame Delphine* features "a more incisive and exact manner of writing" than does *The Grandissimes.*[29]

Despite—or perhaps because of—the story's melodrama, the stock characters, the variety of dialect, and the ease with which one can brush past the complex racial and ethical issues, *Madame Delphine* became one of Cable's most famous works. Its popularity was so enduring that it was dramatized more than twenty years after its initial publication (1902), and at least twice (1914, 1919–1921) negotiations were underway to make it into a motion picture.[30] To this day it remains one of the best known works in Cable's literary canon. As is the case with the earlier "Belles Demoiselles Plantation," Cable no doubt would have appreciated the irony of a story with a strong moral dimension remaining popular for more than a century precisely because that dimension is readily overlooked.

2

"Floating in the Clouds of Revery": Love and Intrigue at the "Café des Exilés"

IN his 1879 review of the newly published *Old Creole Days*, Charles DeKay declared at the outset that "It would be hard to pick out the most charming from these Creole tales. We might make a beginning by eliminating that called 'Café des Exilés' . . ."[1] Somewhat less harshly, nearly a century later Arlin Turner stated that "In several respects [it] differs from the other" tales in the collection.[2] And although DeKay attempted to justify the "elimination" of "Café des Exilés" by pointing out its ostensibly uncharming technical shortcomings ("relatively to the [other stories in the collection], its plot is less clearly drawn, and its dialogue . . . is less intelligible"[3]), and although Turner noted that, despite its differences, it nevertheless is "recognizably a Cable story,"[4] the impression remains that neither commentator seems comfortable with the inclusion of "Café des Exilés" in *Old Creole Days*. Their reaction is entirely understandable. In several important respects—including the narrative technique, the character types, and the use of a double-threaded plot—"Café des Exilés" shows Cable departing from his customary practice in this, the sixth of the stories to be published. But this departure, far from compromising the quality of the story, renders it one of the most innovative and intriguing of the eight tales of *Old Creole Days*.

The narrative technique of "Café des Exilés" is virtually a tour de force. Whereas the typical Cable narrator is omniscient ("Belles Demoiselles Plantation") or semiomniscient (" 'Tite Poulette"), that of "Café des Exilés" only seems so. He records conversations, probes motivations, and offers exposition of personal lives, but Cable makes it emphatically clear that he is reporting information provided him by another individual. More importantly, that other individual is revealed at the end of the story to have been the hero of "Café des Exilés," Major Galahad Shaughnessy: "Only yesterday I\dined with the Shaughnessys—fine old couple and handsome. Their children sat about them and entertained me most pleasantly. But there isn't one can tell a tale as their father can—'twas he told me this one . . ."(116–17) By involving the narrator in the action of "Café des Exilés," even in so peripheral a fashion, Cable has made him into an important minor character of the story and, at the same time, deflected criticism from two of the most persistent problems in his fiction—his tendencies to sentimentalize and to engage in ethnic stereotyping.

The narrator's special status as a quasi character of "Café des Exilés" is evident in the story's opening:

> That which in 1835—I think he said thirty-five—was a reality in the Rue Burgundy—I think he said Burgundy—is now but a reminiscence. Yet so vividly was its story told me, that at this moment the old Café des Exilés appears before my eye, floating in the clouds of revery, and I doubt not I see it just as it was in the old times. (85)

The repeated "I think he said" is eloquent. Far from being omniscient, the narrator admits immediately to being unreliable, and this situation is compounded by the fact that *his* source of information, Galahad Shaughnessy, may not himself be reliable—a possibility presented openly in the twist ending. At this early stage of the story, however, all that is known is that the rather chatty narrator is blissfully frank about his dubious reliability, and that as a result the story is particularly prone to inaccuracies, editorial slants, and prejudices. This situation tends to pull "Café des Exilés" out of the rather stiff realm of docudrama (a serious problem in Cable's political fable, "Madame Délicieuse") while, paradoxically, heightening the sense that the story is based on historical and political realities. That is to say, in a tale that focuses on illegal activities (gunrunning in the Caribbean, gangland-style murder) and that relies heavily on the twin motifs of concealment and lies, it is singularly appropriate that the storyteller cannot quite recall—or pretends not to recall, or has been deliberately misinformed about—the dates, locales, and people involved. As a matter of fact, Cable's New Orleans contemporaries would be acutely aware that the narrator is wrong on two counts: the events of the story actually took place ten years later, in 1845,[5] and the Café des Exilés was situated on Rampart Street, not Burgundy.[6] In effect, the uncertainty (real or feigned) of the narrator heightens the impression that the story he is telling, at least in its main points, really happened.

As Cable begins to flesh out the character of the narrator, he adds to his unreliability a rather shameless passion for romanticizing: "at this moment the old Café des Exilés appears before my eye, floating in the clouds of revery." Since clearly it is the highly imaginative narrator speaking, Cable has spared himself the possibility of being personally accused of oversentimentalization, while still imparting a romantic aura to the story. Cable takes advantage of this further in the second paragraph of the story:

An antiquated story-and-a-half Creole cottage sitting right down on the banquette, as do the Choctaw squaws who sell bay and sassafras and life-everlasting, with a high, close board-fence shutting out of view the diminutive garden on the southern side. An ancient willow droops over the roof of round tiles, and partly hides the discolored stucco, which keeps dropping off into the garden as though the old café was stripping for the plunge into oblivion—disrobing for its execution. I see, well up in the angle of the broad side gable, shaded by its rude awning of clapboards, as the eyes of an old dame are shaded by her wrinkled hand, the window of Pauline. Oh for the image of the maiden, were it but for one moment, leaning out of the casement to hang her mocking-bird and looking down into the garden,—where, above the barrier of old boards, I see the top of the fig-tree, the pale green clump of bananas, the tall palmetto with its jagged crown, Pauline's own two orange-trees holding up their hands toward the window, heavy with the promises of autumn; . . . (85–86)

The passage begins in a straightforward fashion; at first the café is only slightly personified (it "sit[s] right down on the banquette"), but as the imaginative narrator continues, the personification intensifies to the point where the building removes its clothing (stucco). The story's heavy use of the motif of concealment is hinted at in the "high, close board-fence shutting out of view the . . . garden" and the willow that hides the stucco, but rapidly the narrator narrows his focus to the concealed element that really commands his attention—the lovely Pauline D'Hemecourt, daughter of the owner of the café: "Oh for the image of the maiden, were it but for one moment, leaning out of the casement to hang her mocking-bird . . ." If that statement came—or even seemed to come—from Cable, it would be liable to accusations of overwriting. At the same time, it would tend to make Pauline seem almost inhuman—the problem Cable was unable to resolve with the seven daughters in "Belles Demoiselles Plantation" and with 'Tite Poulette. But coming from an admittedly highly imaginative narrator, it seems to be the prayer of a man who has fallen in love with the *idea* of young Pauline. He is so smitten, in fact, that throughout the story he likens her to various commendable ladies of the Bible, as well as to Woman in the abstract.

As the paragraph quoted above suggests, Pauline lives surrounded by a fecund garden. The catalog itself—figs, bananas, palmettos, orange trees—conveys a highly sexual but innocent lushness that is in keeping with her character. It is no accident that she speaks of living in a "fenced city" (99), for her paradise—a word that, as the amateur biblical scholar Cable surely knew, means "walled garden"—is the garden immediately surrounding her father's café. But at the same time that the smitten narrator subtly associates her with Eve, he likens her with almost embarrassing insistence to the Virgin Mary:

Pauline had been to the Café des Exilés in some degree what the image of the Virgin was to their churches at home; . . . She was its preserving influence, she made the place holy; she was the burning candles on the altar. Surely the reader will pardon the pen that lingers in the mention of her. (91)

Even her serving of lemonade assumes an almost spiritual cast:

> [T]he neighbors over the way, sitting about their doors, would by and by softly say, "See, see! there is Pauline!" and all the exiles would rise from their rocking-chairs, take off their hats, and stand as men stand in church, while Pauline came out like the moon from a cloud, descended the three steps of the café door, and stood with waiter and glass, a new Rebecca with her pitcher, before the swarthy wanderer. (92–93)

Coming from Cable, the passage would seem overwritten; coming from his customary ironic narrator, it might be interpreted as ludicrous, even cynical; but coming from this highly imaginative, love-struck narrator, it is the understandable manifestation of his passion. One receives the same impression from this paean to Pauline as the personification of Woman:

> Pauline . . . seemed to [the exiles] held up half way to heaven, they knew not how. Ah! those who have been pilgrims; who have wandered out beyond harbor and light; whom fate hath led in lonely paths strewn with thorns and briers not of their own sowing; who, homeless in a land of homes, see windows gleaming and doors ajar, but not for them,—it is they who well understand what the worship is that cries to any daughter of our dear mother Eve whose footsteps chance may draw across the path, the silent, beseeching cry, "Stay a little instant that I may look upon you. Oh, woman, beautifier of the earth! Stay till I recall the face of my sister; stay yet a moment while I look from afar, with helpless-hanging hands, upon the softness of thy cheek, upon the folded coils of thy shining hair; and my spirit shall fall down and say those prayers which I may never again—God knoweth—say at home." (92)

It is to Cable's credit that although he made the narrator somewhat spoony about Pauline, he gradually reduced the number and length of the impassioned passages about her, ultimately having the storyteller decline to romanticize her further: "but why say again she was lovely?" (113)

As the presentation of Pauline suggests, Cable is able to guide the reader's response to the story in accordance with the narrator's feelings. His adoration of Pauline is so palpable that even when she is involved in the most worldly activities—such as nervously braiding wires while eavesdropping in a closet (107)—our initial impression of her as preternaturally beautiful, kind, and pure is enriched rather than obliterated. The narrator's control over our feelings extends well beyond Pauline. By the time we get to the second page of the story, we have been drawn into the narrator's romanticized account to such a degree that we share with him something of his feeling that "it would set every tooth on edge should I go by there now,—now that I have heard the story,—and see the old site covered by the 'Shoofly Coffee-house'" (86). As a result, our reactions to the exiles themselves, and in particular to Pauline's two suitors, are determined by how the narrator personally—and often prejudicially—responds to them.

The exiles themselves are most unusual for a tale from *Old Creole Days*. Rather than focus on quadroons such as Madame Delphine, or Madame John in "'Tite Poulette," or on French Creoles like the De Charleus in "Belles Demoiselles Plantation" or the Villivicencios in "Madame Délicieuse"—all of whom are lifelong residents of Louisiana and descendants of the earliest families in New Orleans—the characters of "Café des Exilés" are essentially non-native transients. As political exiles from Barbados, Martinique, San Domingo, and Cuba, they perceive New Orleans as a temporary asylum, and as a base from which to conduct their gunrunning. In effect, these Latins have no emotional investment whatsoever in the city, and they do not quite fit into the complex social structure of nineteenth-century New Orleans. For these reasons the narrator—perhaps reflecting Cable's own feelings[7]—presents them with amusement at best, disrespect at worst.

For example, there are two predominant metaphors in the story involving the café itself. One is that it is like a plant that "flowered, bore fruit, and dropped it long ago" (86), and it is specifically associated with bananas, catalpa trees, and corn (86, 87, 93). As the logical extension of this imaginative but rather overused metaphor, the narrator points out that the nonalcoholic drinks served by D'Hemecourt are "a rich variety of tropical sirups"; appropriately, the exiles "came like bees" to drink them (87). The second metaphor, which frankly has nothing in common with the first, posits the café as the "mother" of these homeless exiles: "In the balmy afternoons . . . they gathered about their mother's knee, that is to say, upon the banquette outside the door" (91). The metaphor is strained and overused to a ludicrous degree by the chatty, sentimental narrator, but what is particularly noteworthy about it is its implication: if the café is a mother, then the exiles are children. The narrator in fact is quite explicit about their child-like dimension ("such those exiles seem to me" [86]), and he is so emphatic about their association with bees and children that the reader tends to qualify whatever preconceived notions he may harbor about the nobility and bravery of political exiles. Further, the narrator's presentation of the exiles as bees and children enables him to simplify them almost to the level of caricature. Quite unusual for a Cable story, there are no gray areas of characterization: Pauline is pure womanhood personified; Manuel Mazaro is clearly the villain; and Galahad Shaughnessy is every inch a hero.

The contempt and distrust the narrator feels toward Mazaro are imparted primarily through two emphases: the Latin's dishonesty, and his effeminacy. His stealthiness is suggested at the outset by his "small, restless eyes . . . as black and bright as those of a mouse" (87). Unlike Jules St.-Ange of "Posson Jone'," whose subtle association with a mouse adds to his appeal, Mazaro's association suggests a superficial attractiveness that belies a fundamental wildness. It comes as no surprise to learn that "He could play the guitar delightfully, [while concealing a] knife down behind his coat-collar" (88) or that "it may be doubted whether at any time the curly-haired young Cuban had that playful affection for his Celtic comrade [Shaughnessy], which a habit of giving little velvet taps to Galahad's cheek made a show of" (93). In both word and action, Mazaro is not to be trusted: even the "tear-compel-ling, nay, heart-rending" tales he tells at the café are "palpable inventions" (93). And his insistently negative qualities are only thrown into sharper relief by his effeminacy. The narrator speaks of his "dark girlish face" (87), of his "redundant locks" that "curled so prettily and so wonderfully black" under his white Panama hat (87–88), of his "pretty foot," which he con-templates as he lies to Shaughnessy (100); even the hands that wield the concealed knife are those "of a woman" (88). As is suggested by the presentation of Dr. Mossy in "Madame Délicieuse," it is a serious indict-ment of a male character for Cable to render him effeminate. Between his stealthiness, capacity for violence, compulsive lying, and effeminacy, then, Mazaro is emphatically a reprehensible character. Furthermore, even though we are told that he has some Indian blood (89), it is evident that he is being offered almost as a sterling representative of the Latin exiles as a group, those "harmless-looking" men with "languid, effeminate faces" (111) who "like to lay their plans noiselessly, like a hen in a barn" (94). Cable—or, more precisely, his narrator—clearly is engaged in ethnic stereotyping in its most negative form.

The stereotyping is no less apparent in the presentation of Major Shaughnessy, who clearly serves as the foil of Mazaro, and whose given name—Galahad—is an obvious reference to his masculinity and purity.[8] Unlike the moody and two-faced Mazaro, who turns his "hot thoughts over silently" in his mind "as a brooding bird turns her eggs in the nest" (90–91), Shaughnessy is disarmingly direct and cheery—the archetypal Irishman. He has "sea-blue eyes" that reveal his "boyishness" (88)—not to be confused with the vicious childishness of Mazaro—and that "dance" at the prospect of excitement (105). Shaughnessy sees right through Mazaro's "palpable in-ventions," so "they were never attempted in the presence of the Irishman" (93). He openly acknowledges Mazaro's effeminacy, addressing him as " 'the etheerial Angelica herself' " and " 'sissy' " (99), while still being able to maintain a solid working relationship with him in the alleged funeral society throughout most of the story. But what really cements the reader's favorable impression of Shaughnessy is the simple fact that the D'Hemecourts, *père et fille*, are inordinately fond of him.

Out of all the exiles who frequent his café, it is Shaughnessy whom the elderly, loving M. D'Hemecourt clearly favors. He would speak "long and confidentially" to the Irishman about his only child, and about "the grinding he had got between the millstones of his poverty and his pride, in trying so long to sustain, for little Pauline's sake, that attitude before society which earns respect from a surface-viewing world" (89). Further, it is emphasized that D'Hemecourt—whose Castilian maternity is carefully downplayed— responds to Shaughnessy's Irish personality: "Old D'Hemecourt drew him close to his bosom. The Spanish Creoles were, as the old man termed it, both cold and hot, but never warm. Major Shaughnessy was warm . . ." (88) The kindly old man's fondness for Shaughnessy helps render plausible his sheltered daughter's passion for him; and since the narrator's presentation of Pauline is so positive, when she admits to her father that she " 'would give worlds to think' " that Shaughnessy loved her (98), our favorable impression of the Irishman is crystallized into unqualified acceptance.

Not surprising for a story that focuses upon an idealized young girl and two strikingly different men, there emerges a love triangle: the villain Manuel Mazaro (a Spanish Creole) and the endearing Galahad Shaughnessy (an Irishman) are both in love with Pauline (whose father claims to have both Spanish and French blood). As these nationalities suggest, the resolution of the love triangle assumes a sociocultural dimension that, although not so transparent as the political dimension of the love triangle in "Madame Délicieuse," is nonetheless vital for a full appreciation of "Café des Exilés." The eventual breaking of the triangle and the pairing of Shaughnessy and Pauline is, strictly from the point of view of drama, very satisfying; the idealized Pauline with her aggregate of Biblical associations would hardly be suitable for a man who resembles the "prince of darkness" (110). Mazaro's betrayal of his fellow gunrunners out of jealousy over Shaughnessy and Pauline is very much in keeping with his villainous character, and it seems only just that he ends up in the Carondelet Canal, "cold, dead!," having been ritually stabbed by the gunrunners (116). But because Mazaro is presented as virtually a stereotypical Spanish Creole, his betrayal of the others and his gangland-style execution seem to constitute an unflattering ethnic commentary. As Philip Butcher points out, "whenever there are major characters who are not of Creole extraction in Cable's dramatic personae, the role of hero falls to one of them."[9] In the case of "Café des Exilés," the hero is clearly the dashing, jovial Shaughnessy (as a non-Latin, only he does not take part in Mazaro's gangland execution [116]); and the girl he wins is described as being far more French than Spanish. In effect, Cable seems to be suggesting that the most desirable "marriages"—actual or symbolic—in nineteenth-century New Orleans involve those of northern

European backgrounds, and carefully exclude volatile Latins. One finds evidence of such ethnic distinctions throughout Cable's writings, but it is probably most obvious in "Posson Jone' ": the "Latins" kill helpless circus animals, even though the "northern races were trying to prevent" this (166).

The sociocultural commentary offered by the resolution of the love triangle is certainly present, but Cable does not stress it. For the most part, our attention is focused on romance rather than nationality, and the resolution of the triangle is a major source of dramatic interest. Indeed, Arlin Turner evidently had the romantic triangle in mind when he cited as atypical of Cable the story's double-threaded plot[10] (the other thread is the gunrunning), but in fact the two threads are actually so intimately related that it would be most fruitful to see them as a single, complex plot line.

It was perhaps this complexity to which DeKay was responding when he criticized "Café des Exilés" for having a plot "less clearly drawn" than those of the other stories in the collection; but in fact the criticism is not valid. Granted, at times there seem to be unexplained gaps in the characters' logic (why, for example, would D'Hemecourt and his levelheaded daughter send Mazaro to fetch Shaughnessy, when they are well aware that Mazaro would deliberately hurt the Irishman? [101–2]); but even these gaps are acknowledged (eventually D'Hemecourt "smiled at his own simplicity" for having trusted Mazaro [102]). Generally speaking, there is nothing "unclear" about the relationship between the love triangle and the gunrunning. The illegal operation uses the Café des Exilés as its primary base. It is perfectly reasonable, therefore, that the daughter of the café's owner—herself an occasional waitress—would come into contact with the organizer of the gunrunning (Shaughnessy) and the secretary of the funeral society that serves as its front (Mazaro), both of whom frequent the café as customers. In turn, this double role renders plausible the long, skewed conversation between D'Hemecourt and Shaughnessy, in which the café owner assumes they are discussing his concerns over the Irishman's relationship with his daughter, while the Irishman assumes they are discussing the two "cutthroats" whom the lying Mazaro has told him are waiting for him at the café:

> "Munsher D'Himecourt," said [Shaughnessy], "I'm nor afraid of any two men living—I say I'm nor afraid of any two men living, and certainly not of the two that's bean a-watchin' me lately, if they're the two I think they are."
>
> M. D'Hemecourt flushed in a way quite incomprehensible to the speaker, who nevertheless continued:
>
> "It was the charges," he said, with some slyness in his smile. "They *are* heavy, as ye say, and that's the very reason—I say that's the very reason why I staid away, ye see, eh? I say that's the very reason I staid away."
>
> Then, indeed, there was a dew for the maiden to wipe from her brow,

unconscious that every word that was being said bore a different significance in the mind of each of the three. The old man was agitated.
    "Bud, sir," he began, shaking his head and lifting his hand.
    "Bless yer soul, Munsher D'Himecourt," interrupted the Irishman.
"Wut's the use o' grapplin' two cut-throats, when"—
    "Madjor Shaughnessy!" cried M. D'Hemecourt, losing all self-control.
"H-I am nod a cud-troad, Madjor Shaughnessy, h-an I 'ave a r-r-righd to
wadge you." (103–4)

This conversation (only part of which has been quoted) is extremely confusing to the characters involved; but even so, a multilevel conversation
such as this is certainly not unclear to anyone who has been reading the
story with even a modicum of attentiveness. Further, it should come as no
surprise whatsoever to find that the "funeral society" is a front for gunrunning, and that the coffins of supposedly deceased exiles waiting to be
shipped home are filled wilth rifles instead of bodies. The narrator provides
copious foreshadowing with bemused irony:

> It was for some reason thought judicious for the society to hold its
> meetings in various places, now here, now there; but the most frequent
> rendezvous was the Café des Exilés; it was quiet; those Spanish Creoles,
> however they may afterward cackle, like to lay their plans noiselessly, like
> a hen in a barn. There was a very general confidence in this old institu-
> tion, a kind of inward assurance that "mother wouldn't tell;" though,
> after all, what great secrets could there be connected with a mere burial
> society? (94)

Moreover, the "burial society" members meet at the café after-hours, in a
room behind the café proper, with "the shutters of doors and windows . . .
closed and the chinks stopped with cotton"; the exiles leave the meetings in
a "peculiar way, the members retiring two by two at intervals"; and
M. D'Hemecourt " 'cannot' " tell Pauline why he is unable to close down
the operation of his café (95, 98). This subtle but effective use of foreshadowing is comparable to that of two other "mystery" stories of *Old
Creole Days*, "Jean-ah Poquelin" and " 'Tite Poulette."
    DeKay's second criticism of "Café des Exilés" is similarly questionable:
"its dialogue . . . is less intelligible" than that of the other stories in the
collection, an observation echoed by Arlin Turner: "The dialect is troublesome more than in any of the earlier stories, for the dialogue includes
varying mixtures of Irish, French, Spanish, and Italian . . ."[11] It is true that
these four mixtures are in the story, but in the final analysis they are no more
troublesome than are the dialects in several of the other stories of *Old Creole
Days*. "Posson Jone'," for example, which was published only one month
after "Café des Exilés," features French Creole, West Floridian, and black
dialects, but they are not difficult to comprehend—especially if read aloud.

The one element in the story that seems not to have attracted attention is the twist ending. The fact that the narrator is telling the story as he heard it from the hero implies that anything that might be criticized as a weakness of the story—the unqualified villainy of Mazaro, the disparagement of Latins, the sentimentalization of Pauline—should be attributed not to Cable, but either to the prejudiced narrator who is so self-conscious about telling his story (e.g., they "did what I have been hoping all along, for the reader's sake, they would have dispensed with"—they cried [110]) or to the narrator's unreliable source—a man who "knows the history of every old house in the French Quarter; or, if he happens not to know a true one, he can make one up as he goes along" (117). In fine, the use of a "frame," plus an unreliable narrator with a distinct personality, suggests that in "Café des Exilés" Cable was experimenting with the possibilities of narrative technique. That he did so some years before his better known contemporary, Henry James, is a tribute to Cable's imagination and literary artistry.

3

The Fall of the House of De Charleu: "Belles Demoiselles Plantation"

PERHAPS only *The Grandissimes* is a more enduring work in Cable's literary canon than the short story "Belles Demoiselles Plantation." For more than a century, since its initial publication in *Scribner's Monthly Magazine* (April 1874), it has been widely anthologized and persistently deemed "charming," although few commentators have been able—or, apparently, even willing—to fathom the sources of its perennial appeal. The two critics who have made the most notable efforts to explore the riches of the story are Howard W. Fulweiler and Donald A. Ringe who, although occasionally in sharp disagreement over particulars, share the general belief that Cable is presenting a moral tale that is far more complex than the rather condescending label of "charming" might lead one to believe. Their disagreements stem basically from their disparate efforts to justify what seems to be Cable's failure to incorporate within a logically and aesthetically complete scheme the climactic event of the tale—the drowning of the protagonist's seven innocent daughters. All the foreshadowing, all the geological facts in the world, do not seem to make tenable—except perhaps on the level of the most ghoulish melodrama—the collapse of the beautiful mansion into the Mississippi amidst the "wild wail of terror" (142) of the drowning girls. But no viable analysis of Cable's fiction would seriously entertain the idea that he sought melodrama as an end in itself, nor would it suggest that there were gaping holes either in Cable's logic or in his aesthetic sensibility. By drawing upon the arguments offered by Fulweiler and Ringe, and by approaching the tale as objectively as possible, one can see that the drowning of the seven girls is indeed an integral part of an aesthetic whole—a necessary component in a complex web of thematic and technical, personal and symbolic, elements that few writers besides Cable would have the imagination to create, or the talent to present. And the key to understanding the deaths of the girls—as well as to responding properly to this extraordinary tale—is recognition of the fact that, far more than in most works of fiction, these girls must be perceived simultaneously as flesh-and-blood characters and as remarkably complex symbols. As shall become clear in the course of this analysis, "Belles Demoiselles Plantation" is fundamentally a religious allegory. But thanks to Cable's masterful presentation of the characters, what is at heart a grim and instructive allegory proves also to be one of the most moving and unforgettable stories in American literature.

The first indication of the special allegorical and symbolic position occupied by the seven girls—in other words, the first indication that we are not meant to respond to the deaths only on a personal and emotional level—is the very title of the story: "Belles Demoiselles Plantation." As with the controlling image in a fine poem, the key phrase "Belles Demoiselles Plantation" recurs throughout the story, and progressively acquires myriad associations. As Cable takes pains to point out, the house "had been fitly named" for the girls (122); their identity—and hence their fate—is intimately bound up with the "Mansion" (123) itself and the plantation of which it is the center. In fact, the girls are never seen outside of that context, and so their very desire to abandon their home and move to the city would constitute a symbolic death. Further, the house is identified not only with the seven belles (i.e., the current generation) but with the entire De Charleu family. As Cable emphasizes in a brilliant Faulknerian opening, the original Count had been given the specific tract of land "where afterwards stood" the plantation (121). In effect, the plantation—mansion and land—is identified with the entire family through all generations. It is the House of De Charleu, much as the House of the Seven Gables is the House of Pyncheon, and the House of Usher is "both the family and the family mansion."[1] What we have, in essence, is a careful blurring of identities—those of the girls, the mansion, the plantation, and the De Charleu family. Whatever affects one of the four components will, of necessity, affect the other three. Obvious though this symbiotic relationship may appear, it must be kept always in mind for a proper reaction to the climax of the story. Although the reader is to be shocked at the deaths of the girls on an emotional level, he also is to react to the tragedy—aesthetically, logically, and/or spiritually—as the logical culmination of the degeneration of the family, as the just punishment of ungodliness, and as a means of Christian conversion.[2]

As noted, the key phrase "Belles Demoiselles Plantation"—or simply "Belles Demoiselles"—recurs throughout the story; and, as is to be expected with any entity involving four discrete but interrelated elements, the particular element under consideration at any given time is not always clear. In the following passage, Injin Charlie considers De Charleu's offer to exchange the plantation for the city block that had been left to him:

"Yass! Belles Demoiselles is more wort' dan tree block like dis one. I pass by dare since two weeks. Oh, pritty Belles Demoiselles! De cane was wave in de wind, de garden smell like a bouquet, de white-cap was jump up and down on de river; seven *belles demoiselles* was ridin' on horses.

'Pritty, pritty, pritty!' says Old Charlie, Ah! *Monsieur le père,* 'ow 'appy, 'appy, 'appy!" (139, emphasis Cable's)

In what is (retrospectively) aptly termed "the eulogy on Belles Demoiselles" (141), Cable has deliberately confused the identity of the plantation with that of the seven daughters: "'pritty Belles Demoiselles!'" To acquire the plantation would involve, at least symbolically, the acquisition of the girls; and in fact, dubious sexual relations—so surprisingly common a motif in Cable's fiction—are quite evident just below the "charming" surface of the story. After all, it was miscegenation and bigamy that enabled the family's founder, the original Comte De Charleu, to establish the De Charleu and De Carlos lines; Injin Charlie lives with "an aged and crippled negress" (125); and De Charleu, whose "heavenly" Scottish wife is dead (136), looks back on a life of "mad frolic," "elegant rioting," and dances and quarrels at the notorious quadroon balls (136, 124). Although Injin Charlie's symbolic purchase of the girls would be in keeping with the rather coarse sexual standards of the story, the idea is particularly shocking not only because of the double implications of incest and miscegenation (Charlie is said to be an "injin"), but also because of Cable's distinctive presentation of the belles as preternaturally young, beautiful, and innocent.

Cable achieves their characterization through focusing on three interrelated sets of information: their attributes, their home, and their relationship with their father. As for attributes, the girls are insistently associated with flowers and birds. Indeed, the seven belles are first mentioned in connection with the fabled "century-plant":

> [The family of De Charleu] rose straight up, up, up, generation after generation, tall, branchless, slender, palm-like; and finally, in the time of which I am to tell, flowered with all the rare beauty of a century-plant, in Artemise, Innocente, Felicité, the twins Marie and Martha, Leontine and little Septima; the seven beautiful daughters for whom their home had been fitly named Belles Demoiselles. (122)

The passage is noteworthy for several reasons. First, it is typical of Cable's style. He is able to convey the act of growing by using repetition ("up, up, up, generation after generation") and catalogs of adjectives that, coming rapidly in succession, further convey the quality of steady growth: "tall, branchless, slender, palm-like." Moreover, through the striking use of the liquid consonants *L* and *R* (rose, tall, slender, palm, finally, tell), Cable suggests the apparent placidity of the family—a placidity that belies its origins in embezzlement, arson, lying, miscegenation, and bigamy. At the same time, the liquid consonants may be seen as foreshadowing the watery death of the final generation. The passage is further important in that, as Donald Ringe points out, the century plant blooms only once before its death. As a result, it symbolizes that the family "will soon cease to exist,"[3] although, as shall be seen, I take issue with Ringe's deduction from this element of foreshadowing. In addition to the century plant, the girls are also associated with the "shady garden full of rare and beautiful flowers" (123) that surrounds their home; for example, in the "dumb show" sequence that presents a typical idyllic day at the plantation, the eldest daughter generates "excited comments" by placing violets from the garden in De Charleu's buttonhole,[4] and the twin girls "would move down a walk after some unusual flower" (127). The daughters are also insistently associated with birds: in the evening, "all would be still," and any observer "would know that the beautiful home had gathered its nestlings under its wings" (127).

The girls are further characterized by the mansion in which they live. Cable describes it as having a "broad veranda and red painted cypress roof, peering over the embankment, like a bird in the nest, half hid by the avenue of willows" (123). Of course, the house-as-bird simile serves to reinforce the mansion's identification with the girls ("nestlings"), but more importantly it also conveys a quality of security—false security, as it turns out, for as Cable notes with seeming casualness in the same passage, the house is situated "right under the levee" (122–23). Cable goes on to discuss the mansion at length:

> The house stood unusually near the river, facing eastward, and stand-
> ing four-square, with an immense veranda about its sides, and a flight of
> steps in front spreading broadly downward, as we open arms to a child.
> From the veranda nine miles of river were seen; and in their compass, near
> at hand, the shady garden full of rare and beautiful flowers; farther away
> broad fields of cane and rice, and the distant quarters of the slaves, and on
> the horizon everywhere a dark belt of cypress forest. (123)

Typical of Cable, the descriptive passage is handled organically. Cable's eye (and hence the reader's) moves steadily from the house itself, to its veranda, to its steps. Cable then backtracks slightly to delineate—again, organi-cally—the vista from the veranda: the garden "near at hand"; then, "farther away," the fields; then "the distant quarters of the slaves"; and finally "on the horizon everywhere a dark belt of cypress forest." Taken together, the two descriptions (mansion and vista) offer a striking amalgam of the serene and the sinister. In what we might term the first home/garden sequence, we are presented with the mansion itself. The steps spread broadly, "as we open arms to a child," an image of domesticity and security that is reinforced by the reference to the shady garden that surrounds it. Considerably less pastoral is the second home/garden sequence: slave quarters, and the "broad fields of cane and rice" in which the slaves labor. The third such sequence is quite chilling: there are no homes or people, but only an extensive dark forest. That forest, which "is on the horizon everywhere," betokens not only the Cablesque Nature that is oblivious to man's achievements (and that is evident throughout his fiction), but also the past shame of the De Charleu family. As Cable points out in the story's opening. "the Choctaw Comptesse had starved, leaving nought but a half-caste orphan family *lurking on the edge of the settlement"* (121, emphasis mine). The image of obscure entities existing at the edges of—or just below—attractive surfaces will prove to be a predominant leitmotif of the story.

The massive cypress forest has barely been touched by the De Charleu family; only a tiny fragment of it—enough to make the roof of the mansion—has come under their control, and in a symbolic attempt to deny the implications of the cypress forest, the roof has been painted red. The forest—symbol of the guilt and insignificance of the aristocratic De Charleu family—offers a sinister enclosure that counteracts the ostensibly serene enclosure of the family compound. The river surrounding the De Charleu microcosm achieves the same effect: "From the veranda nine miles of river were seen; and *in their compass"* are the gardens, fields, and slave quarters (emphasis mine). The phrase "in their compass" evidently was meant to function on at least three levels. First, on the most obvious level it is a simple statement of fact: the "majestic curve" (122) of the Mississippi serves as a natural boundary for the De Charleu estate. Closely aligned with this, but on a more symbolic level, "in their compass" of course presents the motif of closure that seems serene, but is in fact sinister. And most abstract of all, "in their compass" calls to mind the four cardinal points—a concept Cable utilizes with striking skill.

Let us return for a moment to the description of the house. It is "facing eastward, and standing four-square, with an immense veranda about its sides, and a flight of steps in front spreading broadly downward" (123). By facing the east and "standing four-square," the house presents one wall to each of the four cardinal points. It is as if it were the center of a compass, a situation that may remind the reader of the Pyncheon mansion in *The House of the Seven Gables*, which has "seven acutely peaked gables facing towards various points of the compass, and a huge, clustered chimney in the midst."[5] Much as the original Pyncheons trampled the rights and feelings of others in their ill-fated efforts to establish themselves in New England— asserted, in effect, that they stood at the center of the world—so, too, the original Comte De Charleu violated the laws of God and man in his efforts to establish a dynasty in Louisiana. As a man quite familiar with the works of Hawthorne—and, just as important, as a writer who could be reasonably sure of his reader's familiarity with so popular a book as *The House of the Seven Gables*—Cable evidently assumed that his audience would make the Pyncheon association, thereby guiding the response to the story. But just as important as the Hawthorne echo in the association of the house with a compass is the simple fact that it faces east: it is oriented toward the traditional symbol of birth and hope—precisely as churches are traditionally placed. The presentation of the De Charleu mansion as a house of worship was no accident. Indeed, the prototype of the De Charleu plantation vividly impressed Lafcadio Hearn as a "temple" and its grounds. Hearn describes a visit to the prototypical home in an 1883 issue of the *Century Magazine*:

> By a little gate set into [the] hedge, you can enter the opulent wilderness within, and pursue a winding path between mighty trunks that lean at a multitude of angles, like columns of a decaying cathedral about to fall. . . . [T]here is a dimness and calm, as of a place consecrated to prayer. But for their tropical and elfish drapery, one might dream those oaks were of Dodona. And even with the passing of the fancy, lo! at a sudden turn of the narrow way, in a grand glow of light, *even the Temple appears*, with splendid peripteral of fluted columns rising boldly from the soil. Four pillared façades,—east, west, north, and south,—four superb porches, with tiers of galleries suspended in their recesses; and two sides of the antique vision ivory-tinted by the sun. . . . It creates such astonishment as some learned traveler might feel, were he suddenly to come upon the unknown ruins of a Greek temple in the very heart of an equatorial forest; . . . (emphasis Hearn's)[6]

Even if the reader were unaware of the resemblance of the original mansion to a religious temple, the details Cable provides are sufficient to enable him to perceive the connection. And an awareness of that connection is vital for our understanding—perhaps even for our acceptance—of the deaths of the seven girls.

Let us consider the ideas presented by the story's two best-known commentators, Howard Fulweiler and Donald Ringe. Both critics acknowledge that there is a strong religious dimension to "Belles Demoiselles Plantation," but they disagree on its precise components and on the end(s) to which Cable presents it. Fulweiler argues that there is a two-sided theme in the story:

> The first and more apparent aspect of the theme is mutability, the precariousness of human institutions and distinctions—social, racial, or economic. The second, and perhaps more important aspect for Cable, the Presbyterian Sunday School teacher, is the Biblical drama of judgment, the inevitable justice of Providence, Whose agents are mutability and nature: time and the river.[7]

Fulweiler goes on to note that judgment in this story "is exacted not only for the sins of the present generation, but also for the sins of past generations,"[8] and that the death of the girls has biblical analogies: "If Cable has suggested God's punishment of Sodom and Gomorrah early in the story [i.e., when De Charleu—like Lot—was famed for "a hospitality which seemed to be entertaining angels" (124)], he suggests finally His judgment of the contemporaries of Noah."[9] Fulweiler's provocative analysis is basically sound, but Ringe takes issue with it, justly noting that Cable's depiction of the plantation is so idyllic that it could hardly be likened to Sodom and Gomorrah: "The imagery [of the story] will not sustain it."[10] Ringe argues that the destruction of the plantation, by throwing De Charleu and Injin Charlie "back upon each other" so that "they meet at last on truly human terms," indicates that the point of the story is the overriding importance of "the ideal of Christian charity."[11] It seems to me that, despite their disagreements, each commentator makes valid points. Fulweiler's argument that De Charleu is being punished for his personal sins and ancestral guilt, and Ringe's argument that the tale is a plea for brotherhood, are both reasonable; but even so, they still do not quite resolve the central problem of the story: Why do seven innocent girls drown? It seems reasonable that the clear association of the mansion with a temple offers a key to understanding the deaths: if the house is being posited as a beautiful pagan temple, then the girls within it (and everything they represent) are "false gods"—all to be destroyed in due course by a self-admitted "jealous God."

An examination of the seven daughters' relationship with their father is vital for the understanding of Cable's complex religious allegory. Their interaction is presented in its most extensive form in what was identified earlier as the dumb-show sequence. It reads as follows:

> To those, who, by whatever fortune, wandered into the garden of Belles Demoiselles some summer afternoon as the sky was reddening towards evening, it was lovely to see the family gathered out upon the tiled pavement at the foot of the broad front steps, gayly chatting and jesting, with that ripple of laughter that comes so pleasingly from a bevy of girls. The father would be found seated in their midst, the centre of attention and compliment, witness, arbiter, umpire, critic, by his beautiful children's unanimous appointment, but the single vassal, too, of seven absolute sovereigns.
>
> Now they would draw their chairs near together in eager discussion of some new step in the dance, or the adjustment of some rich adornment. Now they would start about him with excited comments to see the eldest fix a bunch of violets in his button-hole. Now the twins would move down a walk after some unusual flower, and be greeted on their return with the high pitched notes of delighted feminine surprise.
>
> As evening came on they would draw more quietly around their paternal centre. Often their chairs were forsaken, and they grouped themselves on the lower steps, one above another, and surrendered themselves to the tender influences of the approaching night. At such an hour the passer on the river . . . would hear the voices of the hidden group rise from the spot in the soft harmonies of an evening song; swelling clearer and clearer as the thrill of music warmed them into feeling, and presently joined by the deeper tones of the father's voice; then, as the daylight

passed quite away, all would be still, and he would know that the beautiful home had gathered its nestlings under its wings. (126–27)

The seven daughters are depicted as attractive, charming, giggly, excitable—and rather flighty. In light of the first qualities, the father's adoration of them is entirely comprehensible; small wonder that they manipulate De Charleu with alarming ease, especially since they are to carry on their proud father's bloodline. But the last quality—their flightiness—renders unfortunate the father's submission to their whims. He is "the single vassal . . . of seven absolute sovereigns," an unhealthy relationship that effectively clouds the sound judgment one would expect of a "paternal centre." Immediately after Cable's leisurely three-paragraph dramatization of a typical day at Edenic Belles Demoiselles, Cable counters the scene with a one-sentence paragraph:

And yet, for mere vagary, it pleased them not to be pleased. (128)

The girls are not satisfied. Even an apparently perfect existence on the plantation is not adequate: "If a north wind blew, it was too cold to ride. If a shower had fallen, it was too muddy to drive. In the morning the garden was wet. In the evening the grasshopper was a burden." (131) Despite the attractions of the theater and the masquerades (132), Cable makes it clear that in fact it is "mere vagary"—what Poe might term the Imp of the Perverse—that impels the daughters to demand the move to the city. Despite his occasional efforts to present De Charleu and his daughters in a cozy domestic light, Cable with far greater frequency depicts the girls as fickle godlike creatures and the father as their worshiper—the agent who is meant to satisy their desires, regardless of the motives (or lack thereof) behind them. In fact, the text at times seems overloaded with the diction of sovereignty, and in particular of pagan worship. In addition to the passage cited above, the girls are said to be De Charleu's "feminine rulers" (136); the father feels "unbounded idolatry" for his daughters, who are described as "seven goddesses" (124). And in a two-paragraph sequence clearly designed in part as foreshadowing, De Charleu sees some of the river bank cave in: he cries " 'My God!' " and immediately hears the "joyous, thoughtless laughter of the fair mistresses of Belles Demoiselles" (137). The presentation of the daughters as deities—although obviously partly intended to bestow charm on the girls—has a sacrilegious edge that is too insistent to have been fortuitous.

If the identification of seven pretty, giggling young girls as pagan deities seems strained, one must recall the earlier point that the identities of the daughters, the mansion, the plantation, and the entire De Charleu family have been deliberately merged. Pulled out of context, the phrase "belles demoiselles" can refer to any or all of the four entities; and the implication of this interchangeability is that when De Charleu is said to love "nothing but himself, his name, and his motherless children" (124), he really is talking about one thing. His worship of his daughters, then, is simultaneously the worship of his material wealth, of his family, and of himself—to the exclusion of any other thing or person, including God. Clearly this is conduct unbecoming a Christian. As a Sunday school teacher and biblical scholar, Cable would be well aware of the following passage from the Protestant Episcopal Holy Communion service:

> Hear what our Lord Jesus Christ saith.
> Thou shalt love the Lord thy God with all thy heart, and with all thy soul, and with all thy mind. This is the first and great commandment. And the second is like unto it; Thou shalt love thy neighbour as thyself. On these two commandments hang all the Law and the Prophets.[12]

As Fulweiler would probably agree, De Charleu has flagrantly violated the first commandment. De Charleu's heart, soul, and mind are focused on everything but God. And as Ringe would agree, De Charleu also has violated the second one. The only "neighbour" with whom he has any sort of contact is Injin Charlie, and they studiously avoid intimacy by speaking in English, "an admirable medium of communication, answering, better than French could, a similar purpose to that of the stick which we fasten to the bit of one horse and breast-gear of another, whereby each keeps his distance" (125). Simply by the violation of the two commandments upon which "hang all the Law and the Prophets," De Charleu is, in a manner of speaking, riding for a fall. Even De Charleu seems to recognize this, as he considers his personal past:[13]

> It was hardly worthy to be proud of. All its morning was reddened with mad frolic, and far toward the meridian it was marred with elegant rioting. Pride had kept him well-nigh useless, and despised the honors won by valor; gaming had dimmed prosperity; death had taken his heavenly wife; voluptuous ease had mortgaged his lands; *and yet* his house still stood, his sweet-smelling fields were still fruitful, his name was fame enough; and yonder and yonder, among the trees and flowers, like angels walking in Eden, were the seven goddesses of his only worship (136, emphasis mine)

The "and yet" is eloquent. It is as if De Charleu cannot comprehend how a just God would permit his family to flourish under such despicable circumstances, and in fact it is in the very next sentence that we learn that God is not "permitting" anything. "Just then a slight sound behind him brought him to his feet":

> He plunged down the levee and bounded through the low weeds to the edge of the bank. It was sheer, and the water about four feet below. He

did not stand quite on the edge, but fell upon his knees a couple of yards away, wringing his hands, moaning and weeping, and staring through his watery eyes at a fine, long crevice just discernible under the matted grass, and curving outward on either hand toward the river.

"My God!" he sobbed aloud; "my God!" and *even while he called, his God answered*: the tough Bermuda grass stretched and snapped, the crevice slowly became a gape, and softly, gradually, with no sound but the closing of the water at last, a ton or more of earth settled into the boiling eddy and disappeared. (137, emphasis mine)

As the italicized passage indicates, De Charleu *does* live in a God-directed, highly moral world. Consequently, the flourishing of his family over several generations was more apparent than real. The Lord was, in a manner of speaking, biding His time until the meting out of justice would have its greatest impact. In light of this, the reference to the century plant—rather than suggesting that "the family has run its natural course,"[14] as Ringe argues—signifies the infinite patience with which the Lord waits for the ideal moment of punishment. It required decades of waiting, but the manifold crimes of the original Comte, and the personal sins of De Charleu, are punished in a moment with the destruction of the plantation and the drowning of the seven daughters. And if it seems inordinately cruel for Him to destroy seven innocent girls, one must remember the following passage from Exodus: " . . . I the Lord your God am a jealous God, visiting the iniquity of the fathers upon the children to the third and the fourth generation of those who hate me" (20:4). God's vow to punish a sinner's children would lose all its impact if He qualified it by adding "unless, of course, the children are not wanton sinners." The vow has substance only if it demands the punishment of those who are themselves utterly blameless—and "blameless" the daughters certainly are. There is no indication whatsoever that they have ever done anything that might be construed as a sin or a crime—surely nothing that would deserve a violent death. And if indeed their father perceived them as pagan goddesses, it certainly was not the result of design on their part. Further, as Ringe points out, "five of the seven girls have names with strong positive connotations. Artémise, Innocente, and Felicité suggest only virtue and happiness, while Marie and Martha, the twins, surely suggest the Mary and Martha who are the friends of Jesus in the New Testament."[15] And Cable further underscores the girls' innocence in his masterful handling of the story's climax. Realizing that within only three months his plantation will have entirely caved into the Mississippi, De Charleu brings Injin Charlie to the estate in order to confirm the exchange of "Belles Demoiselles" for the city block:

After a time they struck a path approaching the plantation in the rear, and a little after, passing from behind a clump of live-oaks, they came in sight of the villa. It looked so like a gem, shining through its dark grove,

so like a great glow-worm in the dense foliage, so significant of luxury
and gayety, that the poor master, from an overflowing heart, groaned
again. (141)

Significantly, De Charleu and Injin Charlie see the mansion from "the rear,"
that is, the west—the cardinal point traditionally associated with death. It is
but one more instance of foreshadowing, a device Cable uses with striking
skill and frequency throughout the story (a remarkable early example: the
girls said that the slippery floor of the mansion "would some day be the
death of the whole seven" [132]). Further, the fact that the girls are being
observed from behind, as it were, and without their knowledge suggests
that De Charleu and Injin Charlie are engaging in benevolent voyeurism.
Typical of Cable's practice, these two men are observing individuals who are
helpless and innocent; the voyeurs are deeply concerned over the well-being
of those observed; and neither man can avert the tragedy that befalls the
people they are watching. Indeed, in light of Cable's practice throughout
Old Creole Days, the very fact that he chose to use the benevolent voyeur
motif in "Belles Demoiselles Plantation" constitutes foreshadowing: the
girls are doomed.

Cable also is careful to use two striking similes in his presentation of the
climactic scene—the house "looked so like a gem, so like a great glowworm in the dense foliage." The similes' vehicles (gem, glowworm) share
one feature: brilliance. And to underscore that quality of brilliance—to
bring it out in further relief, as it were—Cable emphasizes the dark backgrounds of the gem and the glowworm: the grove and foliage. In part,
Cable is resurrecting the element of sinister enclosure, the motif of threatening entities that lurk on the edge of seemingly secure and attractive places;
but more than this, he is, in effect, "spotlighting" the house. By utilizing
this device from the theater, Cable is riveting our attention on the doomed
house and its occupants, while simultaneously emphasizing the inevitability
of what is to happen. It is as if Cable is presenting yet another dumb show,
with the girls as actresses helplessly following a script.[16]

The climactic scene continues:

> The Colonel only drew his rein, and, dismounting mechanically, con-
> templated the sight before him. The high, arched doors and windows
> were thrown wide to the summer air; from every opening the bright light
> of numerous candelabra darted out upon the sparkling foliage of magno-
> lia and bay, and here and there in the spacious verandas a colored lantern
> swayed in the gentle breeze. A sound of revel fell on the ear, the music of
> harps; and across one window, brighter than the rest, flitted, once or
> twice, the shadows of dancers. But oh! the shadows flitting across the
> heart of the fair mansion's master! (141)

Cable carefully maintains the quality of theatricality. As a member of the
"audience," De Charleu is locked into the role of helpless observer just as

completely as his daughters are locked into the roles of actresses. He dismounts "mechanically," as if he realizes it is not his prerogative either to participate in the spotlighted action or to leave the "theater." Further, Cable notes that De Charleu "contemplated the sight before him," and then goes on to offer a catalog of the sensory images that De Charleu—the audience—receives. In effect, Cable is carefully describing the stage set and lighting: doors, windows, candelabra, lanterns. Then it is as if the action begins. One hears the "sound of revel" and the harps, one sees the shadows of the dancers across one window: "But oh! the shadows flitting across the heart of the fair mansion's master!" The passage is strikingly similar to what Edgar Allan Poe depicts in "The Haunted Palace," a poem first published in the *Museum* magazine in April 1839:

I.

In the greenest of our valleys,
  By good angels tenanted,
Once a fair and stately palace—
  Radiant palace—reared its head
.   .   .   .

III.

Wanderers in that happy valley
  Through two luminous windows saw
Spirits moving musically
  To a lute's well-tunèd law:
.   .   .   .

V.

But evil things, in robes of sorrow,
  Assailed the monarch's high estate;
.   .   .   .
And, round about his home, the glory
  That blushed and bloomed
Is but a dim-remembered story
  Of the old time entombed.[17]

In his elaborate conceit, Poe is depicting the head of a mentally stable individual; the "two luminous windows," for example, are his eyes. And although Cable has modified Poe's conceit by speaking of De Charleu's heart (a Hawthornesque touch) instead of his head, the fact remains that Cable seems to have had "The Haunted Palace" in mind as he wrote the story's climactic scene. This Poe connection is vital for several reasons. First, in stanza V of "The Haunted Palace," the mentally stable individual goes insane, much as De Charleu loses his mind after witnessing the destruction of his home and family; in that respect, the echo of "The Haunted Palace" constitutes foreshadowing. Second, although "The Haunted Palace" was originally published independently in a periodical, it became widely known to the general public when Poe incorporated it into one of his best known tales, "The Fall of the House of Usher." Although English critic Edmund Gosse bemoaned the similarity of the endings of "Belles Demoiselles Plantation" and "The Fall of the House of Usher"—"for readers of Poe the similarity destroys the necessary shudder of surprise"[18]—I believe that Cable was counting on his readers' recognition of the "Usher" connections: the focus on a mansion, the collapse of the mansion into a body of water, the device of the fissure (in Cable, "the crevice [in the river bank that] slowly became a gape" [137]), the dying out of a once-proud family, and Poe's insistence that the phrase "House of Usher" refers both to the family and its ancestral home. An awareness of the similarities between "Usher" and "Belles Demoiselles Plantation," far from spoiling Cable's story, significantly enhances it.

It is highly unlikely that Cable's indebtedness to Poe was limited to specific borrowings from particular stories. In fact, it is entirely possible that Cable's general fondness for theatricality and his passion for using dense, highly poetic language may owe much to the example of Poe. Both elements come into play when the De Charleu mansion is destroyed:

> The Colonel tossed his hands wildly in the air, rushed forward a step or two, and giving one fearful scream of agony and fright, fell forward on his face in the path. Old Charlie stood transfixed with horror. Belles Demoiselles, the realm of maiden beauty, the home of merriment, the house of dancing, all in the tremor and glow of pleasure, suddenly sunk, with one short, wild wail of terror—sunk, sunk, down, down, down, into the merciless, unfathomable flood of the Mississippi. (142)

Interestingly, Cable guides the response of the reader to the story's climax by focusing initially not on the event itself, but on the two observers' reactions to the event: De Charleu's highly dramatic, intensely physical behavior and Injin Charlie's numbness effectively run the gamut of possible emotional reactions to the scene. Then the scene itself is brilliantly depicted in one remarkable sentence. The first portion of the sentence consists of a catalog of three parallel phrases: "the realm of maiden beauty, the home of merriment, the house of dancing." In this last fond look at Belles Demoiselles, the catalog eloquently recapitulates the charming characteristics of the girls that Cable has reiterated throughout the story—their collective appearance (beauty), personality (merry), and behavior (dancing). In fact, the very sound of the catalog—featuring a wide variety of mono- and polysyllabic words, plus a surprising range of consonant and vowel sounds—betokens lushness and life. These elements are continued in the next phrase, "all in the tremor and glow of pleasure," which more graphically conveys the sensuality—indeed, the innocent sexuality—that is detectable in the catalog. But then Cable introduces the second part of the sentence with the phrase "suddenly sunk"; the unanticipated alliteration (and in particular because it involves the sinister-sounding *S*) marks an abrupt change in writing style that underscores the equally abrupt change in the girls' situation. Particularly noteworthy features of the stylistic shift include the almost exclusive use of monosyllables, plus a heavy reliance on repetition and onomatopoeia; all are interrelated. To be specific, immediately following the pivotal phrase "suddenly sunk" are the words "with one short, wild wail of terror—sunk, sunk, down, down, down." The hammering effect produced by the monosyllables conveys the irresistibility of the tragedy; there is absolutely no sense of a struggle. However, there is a strong sense of downward movement, thanks to the onomatopoeic effect created by the repetition of the words "sunk" and "down." Then, just as suddenly as Cable introduced the second part of the sentence, he shifts to the third: "into the merciless, unfathomable flood of the Mississippi." The reintroduction of comparatively complex polysyllabic words signals the immensity and inscrutability of the river that is able to swallow up a mansion, seven girls, and a plantation without a trace. Further, Cable relies heavily upon words using the liquid consonants *L* and *R* to underscore the liquidity of the river, and he structures the entire sentence in such a way that it ends with the mention of the single most important factor in the story: the Mississippi.

The organic quality of the writing style as the sentence shifts the focus sequentially from the girls, to the sinking, to the river itself, is remarkably effective. Similarly effective is the complete lack of transition into the next paragraph:

> Twelve long months were midnight to the mind of the childless father; when they were only half gone, he took [to] his bed; and every day, and every night, old Charlie, the "low-down," the "fool," watched him tenderly, tended him lovingly, for the sake of his name, his misfortunes, and his broken heart. (142–43)

Cable leaves it to the reader to imagine Injin Charlie taking De Charleu back with him to New Orleans in order to care for him in his homelessness and mental impairment. In its stead, Cable focuses on the passage of time: "Twelve long months," "every day, and every night." The emphasis on the passage of time dramatically underscores the loving dedication of Injin Charlie, who before the tragedy led a life of what Louis D. Rubin, Jr., aptly terms "lazy corruption and sybaritism". "He represent[ed] very much the same image of decay and unregenerate hedonism" that one finds in the world of Cable's " 'Sieur George."[19] The dramatic change in Injin Charlie—the emergence of his sense of charity—is signified by the ironic use of quotation marks around "low-down" and "fool"; likewise, the polyptoton illustrated in the phrase "watched him tenderly, tended him lovingly" further emphasizes the compassionate side of Injin Charlie that previously had been concealed. Moreover, the emphasis on the passage of time proves clearly that time per se does not "heal all"—or at least not for De Charleu, whose misery is eloquently conveyed by the oxymoron, "childless father." In fact, the text in this final scene of the story is striated with references not to healing, but to fragmentation: De Charleu has a "broken heart"; the evergreen vine Charlie brought back from the "caving bank" of the plantation scatters "silver fragments" of light on the floor; De Charleu has a "wrecked body" to match his wrecked mind (143). And yet, this final scene—which unfortunately is readily overshadowed by the powerful climax that immediately precedes it—proves to be overwhelmingly peaceful and satisfying. Partly this is the result of our reappraisal of Injin Charlie; but primarily it is due to the clear emergence of the Christian allegory that was detectable—but never insisted upon—prior to this all-important final scene. The evergreen vine that Injin Charlie salvaged from the wreck of the world of Belles Demoiselles is a traditional symbol of life everlasting, and Cable goes to great lengths to present it as the central image of this final scene. In fact, we learn that De Charleu had noticed the evergreen for " 'many weeks' " (144) before he first spoke to Injin Charlie—that is, even in his delirium. In light of this, it is a major breakthrough in the story when De Charleu says, " 'Send for a priest' " (144). His desire for last rites signifies less his recognition of imminent death than his conversion to Christianity:

> The priest came, and was alone with him a whole afternoon. When he left, the patient was very haggard and exhausted, but smiled and would not suffer the crucifix to be removed from his breast. (144)

This is a far cry from the early, worldly De Charleu: "he was bitter-proud and penurious, and deep down in his hard-finished heart loved nothing but himself, his name, and his motherless children" (124). The immediate cause of his conversion is, of course, the deaths of those children. As a result, it may be argued that their drowning is not only the punishment for the sins of De Charleu and his ancestors, plus the destruction of "false gods"—in short, what Fulweiler would term an act of divine justice with the Mississippi as the agent of the Lord.[20] And it is not only (as Ringe suggests) a paean to the ideal of Christian charity. But it is also—and perhaps most importantly—the constructive act of a loving God who uses the deaths of young girls to guide mankind to heaven. It is a motif well known to readers of Stowe's *Uncle Tom's Cabin* (which Cable had read at the age of nine[21]), in which the untimely demise of innocent Little Eva effects conversions in those around her, and it is likewise prominent in the stories of a much later Southern writer, Flannery O'Connor, whose work utilizes violence, disappointment, and death to convert characters to an awareness and acceptance of God's grace and Christian virtues. Cable in fact emphasizes that the belles literally are in heaven (" 'in paradise;—in the garden' " [145]), where their newly converted father joins them after God—not time—has "healed" him (literally, "made him whole") in the only way that matters in a truly Christian world. Consequently, however differently Fulweiler and Ringe approach the story's climax, each man's interpretation is correct: Cable's religious allegory is sufficiently complex to accommodate all that they argue *plus* the fact that the tragedy is the means by which De Charleu—once a sinner and repository of guilt—gains heaven. Strictly from the point of view of Christian allegory, then, "Belles Demoiselles Plantation" offers a sterling example of a "happy ending." But if, even so, the reader reacts negatively to it, then it is probably because of the Catch-22 situation that allegory frequently generates: it is extremely difficult for a writer to create characters who are simultaneously people worthy of our interest *and* symbols or agents of abstract ideas, situations, or forces. Consider Cable's challenge in "Belles Demoiselles Plantation." Despite his apparent efforts to avoid bestowing distinct personalities on the girls (thereby emphasizing their dual function as symbols of worldliness and agents of God), he had to make them charming, innocent, and attractive in order for us to react with proper shock to their deaths. But he succeeded so well on this second score that he effectively sacrificed the first purpose. A close analysis of the story does reveal that it is a Christian allegory—but how effective is an allegory for which one must search and that, when found, is likely to be rejected on emotional grounds? Surely Cable would have appreciated the irony surrounding the endurance of "Belles Demoiselles Plantation." It has remained popular for more than a century precisely because its religious dimension generally has been overshadowed by the powerful drama used to implement it.

The Story of the True Christian(s):
"Posson Jone'"

O F the eight stories that constitute *Old Creole Days*, "Posson Jone'" was probably the source of the greatest anxiety and pride for Cable. Surely it was the most difficult to publish. Even though all of the other seven tales found berths in *Scribner's Monthly Magazine*, that venerable journal refused Cable's broadly humorous rendering of the encounter between a Creole confidence man and a West Floridian backwoods parson. The rejection of an excellent story by a popular writer might seem like a foolish move, but in retrospect Richard Watson Gilder evidently was responding to the unwritten dictates of the genteel tradition—and in particular to the scruples of editor J. G. Holland—in declining to present to the public a story featuring a drunken minister grappling with a tiger in a circus arena.[1] "Posson Jone'" met with a similar negative response from the editors of the *New York Times*, the *Galaxy*, and *Harper's* magazine, whose H. M. Alden declared in 1875 that " 'the disagreeable aspects of human nature are made prominent, & the story leaves an unpleasant impression on the mind of the reader.' "[2] Less scrupulous were the editors of *Appleton's Journal*, who published "Posson Jone'" in their 1 April 1876 issue. From the moment it appeared, a curious transformation took place: far from alienating the "genteel" readership of more than a century ago, "Posson Jone'" quickly became the most popular and critically acclaimed of Cable's stories—a response that, if anything, only increased as the years went by. In 1881, English critic Edmund Gosse said that "Posson Jone'" betokened "new powers and a brilliant promise" for Cable's career as a novelist, and compared Cable's skill in characterization with that of Flaubert; Charles Dudley Warner in 1883 argued that the story managed to reconcile the era's antithetical impulses toward realism and "idealism" in fiction, noting that although the tale offers "a faithful picture of low life," Cable nonetheless has made it "literature"; literary historian W. M. Baskervill declared in 1897 that "Posson Jone'" was "the masterpiece" of *Old Creole Days*; and an *Atlantic* reviewer in 1901 stated that he could "think of no one fitter to stand . . . in the place next to Hawthorne's than the author of Posson Jone' and The

Grandissimes."[3] And although (justly or otherwise) the heady comparisons of its author to Flaubert and Hawthorne have died down, "Posson Jone'" still generates enthusiastic responses from students of Cable. Claude M. Simpson terms it one of his "most accomplished stories"; Louis D. Rubin, Jr. cites it as "one of Cable's best"; and Arlin Turner argues that "nowhere did [Cable] demonstrate a surer hand, and nowhere did he achieve more truly delightful effects" than in "Posson Jone.'"[4] The sureness of Cable's hand is readily apparent in his presentation of such fundamental matters as the story's opening, characterization, folkloric motifs, and theatrical devices. What may be less readily apparent is that "Posson Jone'" is essentially a religious story.

The opening of "Posson Jone'" is usually long for a story by Cable. For all intents and purposes, there are four introductory paragraphs before Cable's focus definitely settles on the protagonist, Jules St.-Ange, and two more before St.-Ange begins to speak; but even so, none of the introductory material is superfluous. The first paragraph focuses on the attitude and current situation of St.-Ange:

> To Jules St.-Ange—elegant little heathen—there yet remained at manhood a remembrance of having been to school, and of having been taught by a stony-headed Capuchin that the world is round—for example, like a cheese. This round world is a cheese to be eaten through, and Jules had nibbled quite into his cheese-world already at twenty-two. (149)

Even in this first paragaph, there is evident the complex primary tension around which "Posson Jone'" is constructed: the clash between Christian and "heathen" orientations, and, more profoundly, the questioning of what is truly meant by the label "Christian." The very name "Jules St.-Ange"— the surname means "holy angel"—suggests that the protagonist is deeply religious in the conventional sense of the word, but this impression is undercut immediately by the phrase "elegant little heathen." As Cable takes great pains to emphasize throughout the story, New Orleans in 1815 was a heterogeneous, non-Americanized, and fundamentally irreligious society that would not accommodate someone like Parson Jones. That St.-Ange and Jones will initially serve as foils is, then, subtly foreshadowed in the identification of Jules as a "heathen." Further, it is significant that Jules acquired his world-as-cheese simile from a "stony-headed Capuchin." Although currently a "heathen," Jules is very much the product of parochial schools; but at this point, all he seems to have retained from this Catholic upbringing are a profound disrespect for individuals of a religious calling (that the monk who taught him is "stony-headed" signifies that Jules perceives him as unattractive and close-minded), plus a talent for twisting truths. What was presented to him as a scientific fact (the world is round, like a cheese) is imaginatively transformed into a justification for his self-indulgent lifestyle ("This round world is a cheese, to be eaten through"). Jules's talent for twisting facts will, of course, serve him admirably in his brief career as a confidence man. Finally, the world-as-cheese simile subtly associates St.-Ange with mice. This association imparts a certain whimsical charm to St.-Ange, while simultaneously underscoring his diminutiveness—and his stature is one of the most obvious ways in which he is a foil to the gigantic Parson Jones.

The second paragraph further suggests Jules's character and situation:

> He realized this as he idled about one Sunday morning where the intersection of Royal and Conti Streets some seventy years ago formed a central corner of New Orleans. Yes, yes, the trouble was he had been wasteful and honest. He discussed the matter with that faithful friend and confidant, Baptiste, his yellow body-servant. They concluded that, papa's patience and *tante's* pin-money having been gnawed away quite to the rind, there were left open only these few easily-enumerated resorts: to go to work—they shuddered; to join Major Innerarity's filibustering expedition: or else—why not?—to try some games of confidence. At twenty-two one must begin to be something. Nothing else tempted; could that avail? One could but try. It is noble to try; and, besides, they were hungry. If one could "make the friendship" of some person from the country, for instance, with money, not expert at cards or dice, but, as one would say, willing to learn, one might find cause to say some "Hail Marys." (149–50)

In addition to clarifying the setting of the tale (the phrase "some seventy years ago" is not quite accurate; Cable places the story in 1815[5]), the paragraph suggests that Jules is much like Jim Powell, the shiftless anti-hero of F. Scott Fitzgerald's "The Jelly-Bean" (1920), part of the "Tarleton trilogy" of short stories set in Georgia. Fitzgerald explains that a jelly bean is "one who spends his life conjugating the verb to idle in the first person singular—I am idling, I have idled, I will idle,"[6] a lifestyle that would be fully appreciated by Jules, who "idled about" New Orleans. Also like Powell, Jules has seriously depleted his family's financial resources. That "papa's patience and *tante's* pin-money hav[e] been gnawed away quite to the rind" indicates that the "cheese" of the world is in fact money—more precisely, money he uses but has not earned. For Jules, authority figures (be they teachers, relatives, or whatever) are fundamentally people from whom one takes things (metaphors, cash)—an attitude that renders plausible his initial determination to fleece the hapless Parson Jones of the church funds. More subtly, this strong initial impression of Jules's mercenary relationship with his father will serve as a gauge by which to evaluate his transformation into "an honest man" (175) in the course of the story. At the opening of "Posson Jone'," however, the emphasis is not on Jules's capacity for honesty, but rather on his being something of a reprobate. The only avenues of self-improvement of which he can conceive are work ("they shuddered"), filibustering, and confidence games ("why not?"). As with so many of Cable's other characters, Jules is at a distinct disadvantage; he has no marketable skills in a world devoted to commerce. But unlike those other characters—such as Madame John in " 'Tite Poulette"—he is conscious of neither shame nor distress. Instead, determined to retain his positive self-image ("At twenty-two one must begin to be something"), he rationalizes that the decision to pursue a career as a confidence man reflects his sound character ("It is noble to try . . .") when in fact it reflects desperation (" . . . and besides, they were hungry"). This impulse to rationalize will be of paramount importance in his discussions of religion with Parson Jones.

This second paragraph also is important for several other reasons. It reiterates Jules's heathenish attitude toward conventional Christianity: success as a swindler is posited as a "cause to say some 'Hail Marys,' " thus signifying that what little Jules retains of his Catholic upbringing (specifically, going to confession) is retained for precisely the wrong reasons. Further, we are introduced to Baptiste, the mulatto servant who is associated with Jules as insistently as "Colossus of Rhodes" is associated with Parson Jones, thereby underscoring the fact that the two white men are foils. Finally, Cable is careful to point out that the story begins on a Sunday morning. As with Wallace Stevens's poem, the simple fact that the protagonist is not where the reader might expect him to be on a Sunday morning—in church—proves to be of tremendous importance in what is essentially a deeply religious story.

In the third paragraph of the story's opening, Cable abruptly shifts his focus away from Jules:

> The sun broke through a clearing sky, and Baptiste pronounced it good for luck. There had been a hurricane in the night. The weed-grown tile-roofs were still dripping, and from lofty brick and low adobe walls a rising steam responded to the summer sunlight. Up-street, and across the Rue du Canal, one could get glimpses of the gardens in Faubourg Ste.-Marie standing in silent wretchedness, so many tearful Lucretias, tattered victims of the storm. Short remnants of the wind now and then came down the narrow street in erratic puffs heavily laden with odors of broken boughs and torn flowers, skimmed the little pools of rain-water in the deep ruts of the unpaved street, and suddenly went away to nothing, like a juggler's butterflies or a young man's money. (150)

This paragraph is vital for "Posson Jone' " on several counts. Most apparent is the simple fact that it vividly offers local color. Claude M. Simpson has argued that "the chief charm of the story lies in the multitude of details that distinguish the locale from a typical Anglo-Saxon community,"[7] and those "weed-grown tile-roofs" and "lofty brick and low adobe walls" were precisely the sorts of details most likely to appeal to Cable's Northern readership. The passage also is important for the simple furtherance of plot; it is the previous night's hurricane (elsewhere termed a tornado) that has temporarily shut down Cayetano's Circus, thereby making possible the tiger-and-buffalo fight in which Parson Jones will have his climactic scene. But even more important is the fact that Cable is carefully depicting *destroyed* gardens: "one could get glimpses of the gardens in Faubourg Ste.-Marie standing in silent wretchedness, so many tearful Lucretias, tattered victims of the storm." The destruction of these once-beautiful gardens seems intended to present New Orleans as a post-lapsarian Eden—a difficult world where one must use brawn or cunning to survive. Two other elements in this third paragraph must be noted. First, that Baptiste interprets as "good for luck" the fact that the sun appeared in the clearing sky is in keeping with the belief in superstition (a "heathen" orientation) that in the course of the story will parallel—and ultimately merge with—the belief in "providences" (a Christian orientation). Also, the simile in reference to the "short remnants of the wind" that "suddenly went away to nothing, like a juggler's butterflies or a young man's money" calls to mind Jules's situation; as a confidence man, he will juggle words and create illusions to replace the money that, he finds, has suddenly disappeared from his life.

Cable continues to establish the distinctive environment of Jules St.-Ange in the fourth paragraph:

> It was very picturesque, the Rue Royale. The rich and poor met together. The locksmith's swinging key creaked next door to the bank; across the way, crouching, mendicant-like, in the shadow of a great importing-house, was the mud laboratory of the mender of broken combs. Light balconies overhung the rows of showy shops and stores open for trade this Sunday morning, and pretty Latin faces of the higher class glanced over their savagely-pronged railings upon the passers below. At some windows hung lace curtains, flannel duds at some, and at others only the scraping and sighing one-hinged shutter groaning toward Paris after its neglectful master. (150–51)

As with the preceding paragraph about the gardens, Cable in part is appealing to the Northern readership's interest in the colorful world of New Orleans. The opening phrase, "It was very picturesque," transparently indicates this. But the paragraph also helps develop the character of St.-Ange, albeit without referring to him directly. "The rich and poor met together" is a phrase that nicely suggests the financial limbo in which Jules finds himself as the impoverished son of a wealthy family. Since he belongs in neither the wealthiest nor the poorest neighborhood, it is appropriate that he lives in the comparatively mixed (lace curtains and flannel duds) area surrounding the Rue Royale; he is in his element, unlike Parson Jones who stumbles into the neighborhood by mistake. The paragraph is further important in that it illustrates one of Cable's favorite techniques, the Dickensian personification of buildings and inanimate objects: the locksmith's key "creaked," the laboratory "crouch[ed]," and the "sighing one-hinged shutter groan[ed] toward Paris." As with the flowers of the previous paragraph, the personification of inanimate objects lends a distinctive charm to the story; but more importantly, the technique underscores the fact that the humans do not always act like men. This element will assume particular importance in the climactic tiger-and-buffalo fight. The paragraph also makes reference—once again—to the fact that the story begins on Sunday morning, and Parson Jones will take great offense at the fact that the businesses in the area are "open for trade" on the Sabbath. Finally, there is a fleeting reference to "pretty Latin faces." Quite unusual for Cable, there are no female characters in this story, which thirty years after its publication he would describe as "lonesomely masculine."[8]

After these first four paragraphs, Cable's focus settles clearly upon St.-Ange. We are told that he "stood looking up and down the street for nearly an hour" (151)—the sure mark of a jelly bean—and the "masculine gentility" gave him "pantomimic hints of the social cup" (151). Although they gesture from the doors of cafés, it is not necessarily true that "the social cup" refers to coffee. As may be recalled, the Café des Exilés is unusual because it sells syrups (not alcoholic beverages), and liquor and drunkenness are surprisingly common elements in "Posson Jone' "; even the two black servants imbibe illegally at the local grocery store. That the "masculine gentility" would be getting drunk early on a Sunday morning is very much in keeping with the atmosphere of almost leisurely degeneracy that Cable is trying to evoke.

That atmosphere is further evident in the simple, startling fact that St.-Ange owes money to his own servant. Although "somehow he felt sure he should soon return those *bons*" (151), it is nonetheless true that the ostensible social inferior, Baptiste, is in some ways superior to his master. This will prove to be a pattern of particular importance in the relationship between the parson and Colossus of Rhodes.

Jones himself enters the story in a scene reminiscent of the passage in " 'Sieur George" in which the protagonist causes a small riot by wearing a uniform. Before we even see Parson Jones, we see the Creole neighborhood's reaction to him:

Two or three persons ran . . . and commenced striking at something with their canes. Others followed. Can M. St.-Ange and servant, who hasten forward—can the Creoles, Cubans, Spaniards, San Domingo refugees, and other loungers—can they hope it is a fight? They hurry forward. Is a man in a fit? The crowd pours in from the side-streets. Have they killed a so-long snake? Bareheaded shopmen leave their wives, who stand upon chairs. The crowd huddles and packs. Those on the outside make little leaps into the air, trying to be tall.

"What is the matter?"

"Have they caught a real live rat?"

"Who is hurt?" asks some one in English.

"*Personne*," replies a shopkeeper; "a man's hat blow' in the gutter; . . ." (151–52)

It is symptomatic of the almost childlike amorality of the neighborhood that a crowd forms in the hope that they will see a fight, "a man in a fit," a snake, a rat, or, at the least, someone who has been hurt. This almost ghoulish mentality prefigures the grim scene on the Congo Plains where a mob kills a tiger and buffalo, and it also graphically suggests the questionable zone into which the naive Parson Jones has wandered.

His innocence is evident even in his physical appearance. That "his narrow brow was bald and smooth" (152) suggests that he has led a life devoid of both harsh experiences and profound thinking, and in fact this impression is borne out by his conduct and remarks throughout the story. Further, he is husky ("his bones were those of an ox" [152]) and tall—"of giant stature," in fact; but his size belies his personality: there was "a slight stoop in his shoulders, as if he was making a constant, good-natured attempt to accommodate himself to ordinary doors and ceilings" (152). In effect, the huge, rather simple parson is a perfect foil for the diminutive, worldly Creole, and their sharply different attitudes toward life—and in particular toward matters of conventional religion—prove to be the major focus of the story.

The meeting of Jules and Parson Jones has a strongly folkloric dimension. In what Simpson terms "a beautifully localized treatment of the country-bumpkin theme,"[9] Parson Jones visits New Orleans while doing business for the Smyrna, Florida parish of which he is the rector: " 'It's the on'yest time I ever been from home; now you wouldn't of believed that, would you?' " (153). As the result of one of the aforementioned gusts of wind, his hat has been blown off (hence the crowd scene) and rescued by Jules; and the lost hat has revealed that there sits on top of his head—in true bumpkin fashion—a "large roll of bank-notes" (153): five hundred dollars belonging to the Smyrna church. Since only moments before Jules has resolved to become a confidence man—he expressed a particular desire to meet up with "some person from the country, for instance, with money" (150)—it may seem a bit too contrived that he immediately runs into an obviously naive country parson with five hundred dollars. But as becomes evident in the course of the story, that contrivance—or what will come to be identified as a " 'special prov*idence*' " (154, Cable's emphasis)—is at the core of the story.

In fact it is Parson Jones who terms his meeting with Jules St.-Ange a "special providence," and although the reader's initial impulse is to regard

this as ironic—just as ironic, in fact, as Jones's appraisal of St.-Ange as a
" 'plum gentleman' " (152)—it gradually becomes clear that the parson is
correct. But throughout the bulk of the story, Cable derives considerable
humor from his manipulation of the term "providence"; indeed, at times he
might even seem to be burlesquing the whole religious doctrine of providences. For example, Parson Jones, appalled that the owners of cotton
plantations continue to run them on the Sabbath, attributes "the perplexities
of cotton-growing" to God's disapproval: "there would always be 'a special
provi*dence* again' cotton untell folks quits a-pressin' of it and haulin' of it on
Sundays!' " (154) Further, Cable frequently has his characters blur the distinctions between providences (a Christian doctrine) and signs (a heathenish
one). Baptiste has pronounced it "good for luck" in Jules's budding career as
a confidence man that the sun breaks through the clearing sky, and later that
day the rowdy Spaniards on the Congo Plain have a comparable reaction:

> . . . the sun seemed to come out and work for the people. "See," said
> the Spaniards, looking up at the glorious sky with its great, white fleets
> drawn off upon the horizon—"see—heaven smiles upon the bull-fight!"
> (163)

That individuals of dubious faith can rationalize divine approval for reprehensible deeds (swindling, tiger-and-buffalo fighting) would seem to un-
dermine the very doctrine of providences; and this apparent burlesquing
seems compounded by a series of malapropisms relating to providences. For
example, one of the few "religious" experiences of which Jules has personal
familiarity involved his father. Determined to make " 'one baril sugah to
fedge the moze high price in New Orleans,' " the elder St.-Ange sprinkled
holy water and made the sign of the cross on an average barrel, for which a
customer " 'make a mistake of one hundred pound' " (154–55). Jules interprets his father's being overpaid for the sugar as a positive sign from God,
and as a result, " 'I believe, me, strong-strong in the improvidence, yes' "
(154). Cable's malapropism is singularly appropriate, since virtually everything we know of Jules points unswervingly to his being improvident. A
similarly effective malapropism appears several times at the end of the tale.
Having apparently lost the church funds entrusted to him, Jones is distraught; but Jules—drawing upon his skills in rationalization—tries to show
him the bright side of the tragedy:

> "If I was you I would say, me, 'Ah! 'ow I am lucky! the money I los', it
> was not mine, anyhow!' My faith! shall a man make hisse'f to be the more
> sorry because the money he los' is not his? Me, I would say, 'it is a
> specious providence.' " (168)

The Creole's shaky use of English (specious for special) underscores the
apparently questionable status of the doctrine of providences in this story,

and its status seems not to be much improved when Jules later interprets as a "'specious providence'" (169) his winning of $600 from the judge who permitted Jones to be released from jail. But what especially signifies the questionable status of "providences" is that by the end of the story, Jones—who as a preacher is presumably an authority on the Lord and His ways—is himself not sure if Jules's winning might not be a providence:

> "There's no tellin'," said the humbled Jones.
> "Providence
> 'Moves in a mysterious way
> His wonders to perform.'" (171)

What is especially noteworthy about this passage is that Jones is described as "humbled." For a man who earlier in the story could confidently identify providences (the challenges of growing cotton constitute a providence; being overpaid for a barrel of sugar does not), he has deteriorated to the point where nothing seems sure anymore; he even is unsure if he is a Christian, let alone a minister ("'I *hope* I can still say I am [a Christian]'" (169, emphasis mine). One may reasonably question why Cable is playing with the word—and hence the very doctrine of—"providences," while depicting a parson in a far from favorable light. The key to this seemingly sacrilegious tale comes in the very last paragraph:

> The ways of Providence are indeed strange. In all Parson Jones's after-life, amid the many painful reminiscences of his visit to the City of the Plain, the sweet knowledge was withheld from him that by the light of the Christian virtue that shone from him even in his great fall, Jules St.-Ange arose, and went to his father an honest man. (175)

It takes a third party—the heretofore barely detectable narrator who speaks for Cable—to clarify what might not have been apparent before: in everyday usage, the word (or concept of) "providences" can refer to almost anything that one wishes, whether winning at gambling, pleasant weather for an animal fight, or being overpaid for a barrel of sugar. But "Providence" with a capital *P*—referring both to the Lord and to His signs of approval or disapproval—is far removed from the quality of quasi-superstitious whimsy accruing to "providence" with a lowercase *p*. It is this Providence that informs the story and guides our reaction to it. For despite the broad humor of "Posson Jone'," it is fundamentally a serious religious allegory of two very different men who become better Christians as the result of a (seemingly) chance meeting engineered by the Lord.

As was noted earlier, Jules St.-Ange and Parson Jones are posited as foils. The rather slickly sophisticated Jules, having counted "with his eyes" the money in the bankroll on Jones's head (153), strikes up an acquaintance with him. It is in the course of their conversation that most of their disparate attitudes toward religious matters are revealed. Philip Butcher has justly argued that the minister is "a genuinely devout man," but less convincing is his assertion that Jones is "untainted by hypocrisy."[10] There is a certain naive smugness in Jones's appraisal of Jules's account of his father and the sugar-barrel incident: " ' . . . I don't think that was right. I reckon you must be a plum Catholic' " (155). Even less appealing is his flagrant hedging in regard to keeping holy the Sabbath. Following the breakfast he shares with Jules after the rescue of the hat, he asserts that "his conscience" (157) will not permit him to buy coffee to drink on Sunday—although he would be quite willing to be given some by acquaintances (158). He then asserts that he cannot go to drink coffee at the home of Jules's friends because " 'I never visit on Sundays' "—" 'Exceptin' sometimes amongst church-members' " (158). The questionings and rationalizations of "the seductive St.-Ange" (158) continue to illuminate gradually the shaky areas of the spiritual naiveté of "the weak giant," Parson Jones. Even Jones's ingenuously self-assured inquiry as to whether Jules believes he has " 'any shore hopes of heaven' " is met with a disarming, almost blasphemous response from the Creole:

> "Yass!" replied St.-Ange; "I am sure-sure. I thing everybody will go to heaven. I thing you will go, *et* I thing Miguel will go, *et* Joe—everybody, I thing—*mais*, hof course, not if they not have been christen'. Even I thing some niggers will go." (159)

The rather innocent positivism of the "elegant little heathen" has considerable appeal. There is no hint of smugness or hedging in the code by which he lives: " 'What a man thing is right, *is right*; 'tis all 'abit. A man muz nod go again' his conscien' " (158, emphasis Cable's). If one were to strip away the "heathenism" and cosmopolitanism of St.-Ange, plus the naive self-assurance and religious conventionality of Parson Jones, one would find that in their hearts they are "Christians" in the purest sense of the term. Cable's story is, fundamentally, the record of the stripping-away process, and the two men's growing awareness of their mutual Christian love.

The first major stage in the stripping-away process is the early conversation between Jules and Parson Jones. Their remarks reveal the dubious quality of conventional religious terms and doctrines (such as "providences") when used in daily life, and they clarify the weaknesses of Jone's almost self-righteous attitude as a Christian. The second major stage is the visit to the gambling den. Apparently made uncomfortable by Jules's probings of his religious beliefs and practices, Jones declares that he ought to be in church, and Jules obligingly takes him to "a broad, heavy, white brick edifice" surrounded by children (160). Neither a church nor the local "Sabbath-school," the building proves to be "a theatre, honey-combed with gambling-dens" (160). At this stage of the story, Jules is still bent on being a confidence man, and his basic dishonesty is conveyed in the falsetto voice that he assumes whenever he is denying an unpleasant reality (161). Likewise, Parson Jones is still attempting to maintain his crumbling self-image as a man of the cloth who knows nothing of such sinful activities as gambling and drinking. Of course this is not true; he knows a bad hand at cards when he sees one, and his denials only damn him more: " 'No saw! I on'y said I didn't think you could get the game on them cards. 'Sno such thing, saw! I do *not* know how to play!' " (161) Likewise, he terms the "lemonade" in the gambling den " 'the most notorious stuff I ever drank' " (161), a remark that is illuminated by his earlier inadvertent acknowledgment of his drinking (" ' . . . I never [have] taken a drop, exceptin' for chills, in my life . . .' " [156]). The parson doth protest too much. And his determination to extricate himself from the temptations of gambling fall on unappreciative ears in the heathenish world of New Orleans:

> "It's no use; it's a matter of conscience with me, Jools."
> "*Mais oui!* 'tis a matt' of conscien' wid me, the same." (161)

As with the word "providence," Cable plays with "conscience" throughout the story. St.-Ange's remark demonstrates that the word can be used to justify questionable acts by improperly motivated people, and as a result Cable is implying that it has meaning only when coming from someone whose character has been tested. That test comes in the third major stage of the stripping-away process: the scene at the tiger-and-buffalo fight.

How the parson comes to be at the site of Cayetano's Circus, and even more drunk than he was at the gambling den, are matters Cable does not disclose. The previous scene at the gambling den ended abruptly; the parson, having naively agreed to let Jules gamble with the church funds on the condition that he leave without his winnings, reaches for the bankroll but finds it gone. The shock of his discovery is heightened by Cable's reduction of the parson to his hand:

> All was still. The peeping children could see the parson as he lifted his hand to his breast-pocket. There it paused a moment in bewilderment, then plunged to the bottom. It came back empty, and fell lifelessly at his side. (162)

After the parson faints, Jules swears "by all his deceased relatives, first to Miguel and Joe, and then to the lifted parson, that he did not know what had become of the money 'except if' the black man had got it" (162). His desire to be a swindler is still intact, but he has been outmaneuvered—just as Jones has been saved from his own weaknesses—by the intervention of the parson's black manservant, Colossus of Rhodes. Colossus functions as a type of guardian angel in the story; he is an agent of Providence who facilitates Jules and Jones's emergence as honest men, and his lurking about the site of the animal fight—("and there is—but he vanishes—Colossus" [163])—suggests that he is overseeing the testing of the character of both men.

Cable is careful to have the testing take place in an emphatically non-Christian setting. The "rude amphitheatre" where the tiger-and-buffalo fight will occur is filled with a cross section of middle- and lower-class New Orleans. Especially evident are those in "the lowest seats":

> The lowest seats were full of trappers, smugglers, Canadian *voyageurs*, drinking and singing: *Américains*, too—more's the shame—from the upper rivers—who will not keep their seats—who ply the bottle, and who will get home by and by and tell how wicked Sodom is; . . .
> The afternoon is advancing, yet the sport, though loudly demanded, does not begin. The *Américains* grow derisive and find pastime in gibes and raillery. They mock the various Latins with their national inflections, and answer their scowls with laughter. Some of the more aggressive shout pretty French greetings to the women of Gascony, and one bargeman, amid peals of applause, stands on a seat and hurls a kiss to the quadroons. (163–64)

In the midst of this "Sodom," there suddenly is seen "a man [who] is standing and calling—standing head and shoulders above the rest—calling in the *Américaine* tongue" (164). Thanks to the shift in point of view, it is not immediately apparent that this is Parson Jones. Almost all that is recognizable of the "old" Parson Jones is his height—a height that previously had suggested his being closer to God than are ordinary men by virtue of his being a preacher, but which now, by literally making him stand out in a crowd, is emblematic of the revelation of the all-too-human weaknesses he had tried to deny before. At this point, however, he has yet to realize the implications of what he says or does. "[W]ilder, with the cup of the wicked, than any beast, is the man of God from the Florida parishes" (165), and in his drunkenness his true self emerges. Literally picking up the tiger, he preaches:

> "The tiger and the buffler *shell* lay down together! You dah to say they shayn't and I'll comb you with this varmint from head to foot! The tiger and the buffler *shell* lay down together. They *shell!*" (166)

This curious amalgam of the rhetoric of backwoods "flyting" and the New Testament significantly contributes to the farcical quality of the scene.[11] But more seriously, what the parson says and does is symptomatic of the qualitative changes occurring in Jones and St.-Ange. Even in his drunken state, Jones shows himself to be a preacher in the purest sense of the term. Unlike the statements reflecting naive self-righteousness early in the story, the beliefs he espouses in the arena are from the depths of his heart: *in vino veritas.* Likewise, St.-Ange—although he finds the spectacle "fun" and he "laughed, [and] clapped his hands" (166)—has essentially abandoned his impulse to be a confidence man. Far from wishing to hurt or deceive Jones, St.-Ange "ever kept close to the gallant parson" (166). He stands in sharp contrast to "Joe," evidently his friend and intended copartner in crime, who "contrariwise, counted all this child's-play an interruption. He had come to find Colossus and the money" (166). But Joe does not succeed. The tiger and buffalo are killed by the rowdy mob, and the drunken preacher is taken to the local *calaboza.*

What occurs in the *calaboza* constitutes the fourth stage in the stripping-away process. St.-Ange reveals his Christian desire to help the less fortunate—a desire that has not been evident in his abortive career as a confidence man—by arranging with Judge De Blanc for the parson to be released on a "pass." At the same time, the parson reveals his own heartfelt awareness of what it means to be a Christian by refusing the pass:

> "[F]irstly, I have broken the laws, and ought to stand the penalty; and secondly—you must really excuse me, Jools, you know, but the pass has been got onfairly, I'm afeerd. You told the judge I was innocent; and in neither case it don't become a Christian (which I hope I can still say I am one) to 'do evil that good may come.' I muss stay." (169)

Far from simply talking about being a Christian or making excuses, the parson for the first time is acting like one; and Cable further underscores the strong religious dimension of the scene by having the two men undergo a symbolic role reversal:

> [T]he fountain of [St.-Ange's] tenderness was opened. He made the sign of the cross as the parson knelt in prayer, and even whispered "Hail Mary," etc., quite through, twice over. (169)

The confidence man and his victim—the tiger and the buffalo, if you will— are a vision of Christian peace and love.

The final scene of the story is less a fifth stage of the stripping-away process than a confirmation that the process is complete. The parson boards the *Isabella* to sail home to Florida without Colossus, who is believed to have already left New Orleans. As Jules sees the preacher off, the fact that his Christianity is fully emerged is signified by his generous and un- prompted offer to give the parson $500 of his winnings to replace the lost church money (171–72)—a far cry from the self-centered swindler of early in the story. And Parson Jones's Christianity is further signified by his refusing the offer, preferring instead to ask God's forgiveness for being " 'a plum fool,' from whom 'the conceit had been jolted out' " (173). If the ending of the story seems a bit too contrived, too happy—Colossus emerges from the hold of the ship and places the "lost" church funds in the parson's hat, while Jules resolves to pay his old debts and go to his father "an honest man" (175)—it nevertheless is perfect for the point Cable is trying to make. A true Christian is to be recognized not by his rhetoric but by his actions— actions that reflect what is deep in his heart. That a city confidence man and a backwoods parson have served as the unlikely agents for one another's realization of this point is simply a sterling example of the mysterious ways in which providence (with a capital *P*) works; and it is an idea quite accessible to readers of Flannery O'Connor, who likewise utilizes unlikely characters—the Misfit, a Displaced Person from Poland, a bull—as agents of Christian conversion. And in a motif anticipatory of *The Sacred Fount* and *The Ambassadors*, Cable argues that the "great fall" of the parson facilitated the rise of St.-Ange (175), to the point where they are approximately equal. What Cable's intrusive narrator has identified as "the story of a true Christian . . . to wit, Parson Jones" (157)[12] is thus actually the story of two true Christians—Jones and St.-Ange—each of whom (in Miss O'Connor's words) is a "Christian malgré lui."

What greatly facilitated their transformation was the intervention of Colossus of Rhodes, the manservant of Parson Jones. Colossus is described as "a short, square, old negro, very black and grotesque" (154). This is hardly what one might expect a guardian angel (in *Madame Delphine* termed an "angel guardian" [26]) to look like, but the discrepancy between his appearance and behavior is simply a dramatic example of the Lord's mysterious ways. Much as his namesake guarded the harbor at Rhodes, Colossus guards his master's interests, warning him to be careful of the doubtful-looking St.-Ange (155), urging him not to drink (156), thoughtfully picking the parson's pocket so as to safeguard the church funds (156), shadowing the parson and Jules around New Orleans at a discreet distance (160), and dutifully returning the money as the reformed parson sails home to Florida (174). That he is a divine agent is overtly (if comically) emphasized in the final scene of the story. As the contrite parson prays to God for the return of the church funds, Colossus responds on His behalf by depositing the bankroll in Jones's hat.[13]

Cable's depiction of the spiritual emergence of two Christians is handled with consummate skill. His theme is kept in consistently sharp focus: there are no subplots to obscure Cable's subtle points, and no female love interest to infuse the sentimentality that so often compromised the impact of his stories. As Cable himself noted in 1909, he excluded women from the story so as to "portray an ardent and controlling mutual affection springing into life wholly apart from the passion of sex."[14] Nor are there excessive details: Cable confines the action to four settings—the neighborhood of Rue Royale, the amphitheater and *calaboza*, and the dock—and the action is limited to exactly twenty-four hours, with no flashbacks, no moralizing, and a dearth of exposition. In fact, the story comes across as a well-made play. This impression is compounded by the sudden emergence of the narrator in what is essentially an epilogue ("The ways of Providence are indeed strange . . .") and by the strikingly heavy use of dialogue. By presenting the broken English of a Creole, plus black Southern dialect and the "lingual curiosities" (152) of a West-Floridian backwoodsman, Cable is creating a linguistic smorgasbord that dazzled readers in the 1870s, and that continued to generate interest decades thereafter. Indeed, it was in no small measure the variety of dialects in "Posson Jone' " that made it the most popular work Cable recited in his career as a public lecturer both here and in Europe.[15] The fascinating sounds of the dialogue, plus the aforementioned theatrical elements in the story, made "Posson Jone' " an ideal candidate for dramatization. Charles DeKay suggested it be made into a play as early as 1879, and by 1901 the story was still so popular, and the idea of theatrical success was so appealing to Cable, that he did in fact attempt to make the story into a play.[16] Even though this project did not succeed, the fact remains that the theatrical qualities and broad humor of "Posson Jone' " prevent this tribute to Christian love from turning into a dry Sunday-school allegory. Indeed, the only problem with "Posson Jone' " is that the story's serious religious dimension is too readily lost in the "rollicking fun"[17] of the interaction between Jules and Jones. As with "Belles Demoiselles Plantation," religious allegory and good fiction do not always mix well.

A Fable of Love and Death: "Jean-ah Poquelin"

FIRST published in *Scribner's Monthly Magazine* in May 1875, "Jean-ah Poquelin," the touching tale of a once-prosperous Creole's loving care of his leprous half brother, struck a number of chords in Cable's day. The story was a particular favorite of Samuel Clemens, who enjoyed reading aloud the Creole-English of the title character; indeed, nearly fifty years later William Dean Howells noted that he could not read "Jean-ah Poquelin" without hearing " 'the voice of Mark Twain . . . reading its most dramatic phrases with his tragic pleasure' in the defiance of the old slave-trader."[1] On the other hand, enraged Creoles, notable in the New Orleans French-language newspaper *L'Abeille,* expressed dismay at Cable's choice and treatment of materials;[2] but most readers throughout the world instinctively recognized the tale's excellence. A careful scrutiny of the text indicates that the excellence lies in Cable's unusual talent for providing exposition, for creating and maintaining tone, and for delineating character. Each of these three elements is multifaceted; all interact to produce a literary text so dense and rich that it may be likened to poetry.

Consider the opening paragraph:

> In the first decade of the present century, when the newly established American Government was the most hateful thing in Louisiana—when the Creoles were still kicking at such vile innovations as the trial by jury, American dances, anti-smuggling laws, and the printing of the Governor's proclamation in English—when the Anglo-American flood that was presently to burst in a crevasse of immigration upon the delta had thus far been felt only as slippery seepage which made the Creole tremble for his footing—there stood, a short distance above what is now Canal Street, and considerably back from the line of villas which fringed the river-bank on Tchoupitoulas Road, an old colonial plantation-house half in ruin. (179)

As exposition, the paragraph is perfect. The writing itself is remarkably dense and organic. The paragraph moves steadily from the broad sweep of "the present century," to Louisiana, to New Orleans, to Canal Street, to Poquelin's house—a zeroing-in that not only clarifies the focus of the story (the house will prove to be symbolic), but also is emblematic of Poquelin's situation: put into perspective, his story is but a tiny piece of American history, but no less poignant for that. At the same time that the paragraph steadily brings Poquelin into focus and perspective, it also conveys the sense of activity and turmoil that prevailed at the time the story takes place; that is, the rush of events in Louisiana is suggested by the rush of 118 words compressed into a single sentence. Hence the writing style, in and of itself, provides exposition; but so too, of course, do the facts presented. We learn immediately of the tale's geographic and temporal setting: it takes place in Louisiana, a part of the country still so alien to most readers in 1875 that it might as well have been on a different planet; and it is set "in the first decade of the present century"—a bit of information that is presented with "seem-ing casualness,"[3] but that is so vital that Cable has placed it in the most prominent location possible in his text, the very opening. It is essential that we realize at the outset that "Jean-ah Poquelin" occurs just after the Loui-siana Purchase (1803). By setting the story some seventy years before, Cable accomplishes several things. First, the temporal distancing theoretically deflects possible criticism by the Creole community, although in fact the Creoles took umbrage at the tale nonetheless. Second, the distancing effect heightens the emotions; the heroism and love of Poquelin seem larger than life, much as the crassness and commercialism of the Yankee municipal authorities and businessmen are rendered unbearably distasteful. Third, while at the same time that the people, emotions, and events seem intensely real, there is a never-never-land aura about the story that is characteristic of so much of Cable's fiction; indeed, the original title of *Old Creole Days* was *Jadis,* loosely translated as "Once upon a time. . . ."[4] On the most practical level of narrative technique, however, the fact that the story is set imme-diately after the Louisiana Purchase makes both plausible and comprehensi-ble the acute tension between the newly established American government and the old Creole order—a tension that peaks in Poquelin's personal interviews with the governor and a minor city official, as well as in the abortive shivaree. This tension bubbles just beneath the surface of the text, and it generally assumes one of two related forms: humor and irony. Both are carefully rendered in the opening paragraph. Cable presents not only the historical and cultural situation, but also the tone of his story in his depic-tion of the Creoles "kicking" at a catalog of what he humorously terms "vile innovations." That the catalog itself ranges from the sublime (trial by jury) to the ridiculous (American dances) indicates both the comprehensiveness of the Creoles' scorn and, by extension, the ludicrousness of some of their obstinacy. In the story itself, that ludicrousness will take the form primarily of Poquelin's seemingly perverse refusal to permit his property to be "developed" by Yankee entrepreneurs; but it is in keeping with Cable's acute sense of irony that what the community *perceives* as Poquelin's Creole "kicking" proves to be an all-encompassing, painfully self-sacrificing fraternal love. The humorous tone established in the opening paragraph proves, therefore, to be more ironic than comedic. It provides an intentionally misleading conception of the Creoles as stubborn and unreasonable, and as such it renders Poquelin's initially misunderstood behavior all the more poignant when the truth is finally revealed.

The opening paragraph also introduces the story's predominant leitmotif: water imagery. The water imagery is first presented in Cable's graphic rendering of Anglo-American immigration as a "flood," which at the time the story was set had been "felt only as slippery seepage." The water image not only is a dramatic presentation of a demographic fact, but also is the first mention (albeit subtle and indirect) of the single most important factor in the lives of all Louisianians, including those of "Jean-ah Poquelin"—the Mississippi. This river pervades the story so completely that one might be tempted to overlook it, if not for the fact that one of its marshes near Tchoupitoulas Road is absolutely vital for the characterization of the tale's protagonist. As the story opens, Poquelin lives in his ancestral plantation house in the midst of "one of the horridest marshes within a circuit of fifty miles" (179). Although John Cleman is correct that the marsh, "wild as Africa" (184), signifies the dying Creole way of life and the slave trade upon which it depended,[5] one must realize that the marsh's symbolic dimension is far more complex than this; in fact, the "noxious wildness" (179) is emblematic of Poquelin's personal situation. Early in his life, Poquelin had been "an opulent indigo planter, standing high in the esteem of his small, proud circle of exclusively male acquaintances in the old city" (180). As the story begins, however, Poquelin lives in social and intellectual isolation. He is, for all intents and purposes, an island surrounded by political, economic, and cultural turmoil. His intense love for his leprous half brother Jacques serves, ironically enough, to obliterate any possibility of emotional support from the one group to which he feels closest, and of which the Yankees perceive him to be a sterling example: the Creoles. Unwilling to be pressured into sending his brother to the dreaded Terre aux Lepreux, Poquelin interacts as little as possible with the Creole community in which he had once been prominent. Because he evidently also fears the possibility of transmitting his brother's leprosy to others through physical contact, he avoids all but occasional verbal contact with those around him, shunning even the (literal) helping hand of "Little White," the corporate secretary who discerns the source of Poquelin's aloofness early on. As he interacts only with a mute slave and a doomed brother, Poquelin leads a pathetic existence so lonely and so contracted that it can be likened only to self-imposed exile on an island. The expanse of water that literally and figuratively separates Poquelin from the rest of humanity is insistently symbolic. The "big, ravening fish, and alligators" that hold the canal "against all comers" (180) transparently represent Poquelin, who defends his way of life, his privacy, his home, and above all his doomed little family circle from the Yankee developers, Creole gossips, and malicious adolescents who seek to torment him. By the same token, "The shallow strips of water . . . hid by myriads of aquatic plants, under whose coarse and spiritless flowers, could one have seen it, was a harbor of reptiles, great and small, to make one shudder to the end of his days" (180) suggests that Cable, albeit pre-Freudian, fully comprehended the capacity of a standing body of water to symbolize the human psyche. Poquelin's mind—"could one have seen it"—is a harbor of troubles and torments. Friendless and misunderstood, Poquelin must endure verbal and physical abuse at a time when he most needs compassion. He must deal with the guilt of having taken his beloved brother Jacques to the leprous Guinea Coast on a slave-trading junket, and he must face the simple, cruel fact that, being thirty years Jacques's senior, he will probably predecease him—and the dear brother, no longer protected and loved, will be forced to spend the remainder of his hideous life in a leper colony. Clearly, then, Poquelin's insistent association with water is, paradoxically, both negative and positive—negative in that his personal existence is so utterly constricted by his islandlike lifestyle, but positive in that he chose, and staunchly defends, that lifestyle out of love for his brother. Small wonder that the sympathetic Little White, so moved by Poquelin's voluntary exile, characterizes the bizarre situation as a "nightmare" (200).

Given Poquelin's close association with water, it is not surprising that soil is a negative element in Cable's tale. Early on, Poquelin travels by boat with his mute slave as the rower, but with the marsh drained by municipal authorities and Yankee businessmen, "He cannot be rowed home along the old canal now; he walks. He has broken sadly of late . . ."(192). Like the proverbial fish out of water, Poquelin finds himself helpless on soil; and it is a clod of *dirt* thrown by a mob that characterizes the first direct public assault on the old man. Not surprisingly, the dreaded region to which Jacques must go after Poquelin's death is called the Terre aux Lepreux—the "Leper's *Land*," rather than colony (209).

Much as Poquelin is associated with water, his character is presented through his house. Although Joseph J. Egan is correct that the house "externalizes the decay and approaching death of the Creole order,"[6] it is far more important as a personal symbol of Poquelin. The first description of the mansion states that it was "of heavy cypress, lifted up on pillars, grim, solid, and spiritless, its massive build a strong reminder of days still earlier" (179). Poquelin himself, with his "short, broad frame" (185), is comparable to the "massive" and "solid" house in which he lives. As has been noted, he is symbolically "lifted up on pillars" by forcing himself to remain aloof from the community for the sake of his brother. Finally, the house's appearance suggests that it has seen better days—as, indeed, has Poquelin, who at one time had been "a bold, frank, impetuous, chivalric adventurer" (181). By the same token, the house has "dark, weather-beaten roof and sides" (180) much as Poquelin, during his initial interview with the governor, had a "bronzed leonine face" and a "hard and grizzled" chest" (185). It is also noteworthy that the house early in the tale seems "like a gigantic ammunition-wagon stuck in the mud and abandoned by some retreating army" (180). The militaristic diction carries over into the description of Poquelin, whose eye, "large and black, was bold and open like that of a war-horse, and his jaws shut together with the firmness of iron" (185). The twin motifs of abandonment and retreat should not, however, be overlooked; they suggest not only that Poquelin is voluntarily being left behind by the "progress" occurring in New Orleans, but that his family fortunes are in a type of retreat—stuck in the symbolic mud as the Poquelin estate rapidly is overrun by noxious weeds. Cable is quite explicit that the deterioration of the Poquelins is the result of the weakening of the family itself. While Jean was an adventurer, his brother Jacques was "a gentle, studious, book-loving recluse," and "it was between the roving character of the one brother, and the bookishness of the other, that the estate fell into decay" (181). Cable rescues his tale from possible bathos by making both brothers, the last of their line, all too human; and as their situation worsens, so does the situation of the symbolic house. When last described, just before the shivaree, it is "tilted awry and shutting out the declining sun" (201), a death image that foreshadows Poquelin's death later that night. His demise should come as no surprise. Cable makes it clear that with the draining of the symbolic marsh, Poquelin is suddenly transformed from a vigorous, tanned, and leonine middle-aged Creole into what is simply termed "an old man."

However, the diction of stagnation and death refers less insistently to the dying Creole society or to Poquelin, his family line, and his house than it does to his brother Jacques. Of course, it is in keeping with the Southern Gothic quality of the story that there be a mystery surrounding the concealed relative, and that mystery is conveyed most graphically in the reactions of the townspeople to his uncertain fate:

> Among both blacks and whites the house was the object of a thousand superstitions. Every midnight, they affirmed, the *feu follet* came out of the marsh and ran in and out of the rooms, flashing from window to window. The story of some lads, whose words in ordinary statements was worthless, was generally credited, that . . . they saw, about sunset, every window blood-red, and on each of the four chimneys an owl sitting, which turned his head three times round, and moaned and laughed with a human voice. There was a bottomless well . . . beneath

the sill of the big front door . . . ; whoever set his foot upon that threshold disappeared forever in the depth below. (183–84)

In keeping with the fact that the house is a projection of the character of Poquelin, he, too, becomes a source of mystery:

> . . . he became an omen and embodiment of public and private ill-fortune. . . . If a house caught fire, it was imputed to his machinations. Did a woman go off in a fit, he had bewitched her. Did a child stray off for an hour, the mother shivered with the apprehension that Jean Poquelin had offered him to strange gods. (192)

With typical Cable irony, most of these assertions come not from the Americans in the community—so alien to New Orleans that Cable refers to them in French as *les Américains*—but from the Creole community that would be expected to stand behind Poquelin, especially in a time of culture clash. The mystery itself, of course, centers not on the house of Poquelin, but on the uncertain fate of Jacques. Cable consistently suggests—but never openly states—that Jacques is dead. Cable has townspeople remark that " '*Grief* would out with the truth' "(182, emphasis mine); the "silent question" that is constantly posed to Poquelin early in the story is " 'Where is thy brother Abel?' " (183); and Cable even writes of Poquelin's "apparent" fondness for his brother in their early days (181)—a word that can mean "real and obvious," or "false and only seeming." Even when Little White, the secretary of the dubious "Building and Improvement Company" (Cable's ironic quotation marks) sees Jacques and realizes he is a leper, he reacts in such a way that he could be seeing either a living man or a ghost. Having been instructed by his employers to spy on Poquelin's house, the "mild, kind-hearted little man" (195) visits the decaying mansion at night, "bearing himself altogether more after the manner of a collector of rare chickens than according to the usage of secretaries" (195). That White is reduced to the posture of a common chicken thief suggests not only the low level to which the "Building and Improvement Company" must sink in order to discredit the stolid Poquelin, but also that the Poquelin situation brings out the worst in even the best of men—their commonest, most reprehensible traits. It is important, however, that the secretary does discern the truth. The first indication White receives that the Poquelin mystery is actually leprosy is the "strange, sickening odor . . . loathsome and horrid" (196). It is in keeping with Cable's study of misconceptions, of failing to *see* things accurately, that White first *smells* Jacques's diseased body. Significantly, White terms it "a smell of death" and concludes that "the mystery is solved" (197)—but for him, not the reader, since the rather disconnected observations he makes of the leprous Jacques could apply equally well to a ghost or a leper (leprosy is traditionally termed a "living death"). For instance, the secretary describes

Jacques as being "ghostly white"; he wonders, " 'Great Heaven! can it be that the dead do walk?' "; and Jacques's voice is "unearthly" (196, 197, 198).

The confusion over whether Jacques is a ghost or a leper is essential for the maintenance of the story's mystery; but far more importantly, it underscores the theme already touched upon briefly—that for Cable, things are not always as they appear. The confusion is perhaps most apparent in Cable's handling of the character of Little White. The special function of Little White in Cable's tale is first signified by his distinctive and symbolic name. The epithetic "Little" connotes smallness, inferiority, pettiness, and weakness; and it is reflective of Cable's sense of irony that although White is physically small (as, indeed, was Cable himself) and technically an underling at the "Building and Improvement Company," he is far from being petty or weak. He visits the Poquelin mansion at night, something most locals are too terrified to do except in groups or on a dare. He declares to the corporation that employs him that " '. . . I can't help you to make a [legal] case against the old man, and I'm not going to' " (199). He defends Poquelin from a clod-throwing mob of 150 vicious youths, thereby making himself "a source of sullen amazement" (198)—an act that foreshadows his temporarily successful dissuasion of the shivaree participants from visiting the home of the dying Poquelin, and his subsequent confrontation of them after the old man's death. Likewise, the surname "White" is deliberately misleading. Its colorlessness connotes fear and lack of character, whereas in fact White (even his wife Patty calls him only by his surname) is a man of uncommon courage and conviction. In this regard, he is not unlike Poquelin himself; and it is here that the confusion of identities, a technical device that Cable uses with remarkable skill in *Old Creole Days,* comes into play. Although White has minimal direct interaction with Poquelin (the old man even refuses his help "with a fierce imprecation" when White tries to aid him after a mob attack [199]), it is clear that he is the only member of the community who can comprehend Poquelin's situation; and his emotional proximity to Poquelin calls to mind the leprous Jacques's proximity to his brother. This would suggest that Little White acquires an identity comparable not only to that of Poquelin, but also to that of Poquelin's "little" [younger] "white" [leprous] brother. Cable is insistent that the leprous Jacques is "little" (e.g., 209) and "white," so much so that at times the reader is momentarily confused about whether he is discussing the leper or the secretary. In a story with so few named characters, it is clear that the secretary's name was selected precisely because of its associations with Jacques. Much as Jacques and Poquelin have become outcasts, mere "ghosts" of their former selves, so too the secretary becomes an outcast of the American world he represents. Eventually he is regarded as an object of scorn as a result of his championing of Poquelin: "it was not long before the disrelish and suspicion which had followed Jean Poquelin so many years fell also upon him" (198). As this secretary of the American development firm acquires a Creole identity, it should come as no surprise that in the evenings he and his wife take to "sitting on their doorsteps on the sidewalk, as Creole custom had taught them" (201), and that only he realizes, perhaps instinctively, that the elderly Creole had died on the night of the shivaree.

The irony and confusion that are so apparent in Cable's deliberate blurring of the characters of Little White, Poquelin, and Jacques seem not to have been intended as a negative commentary on any group or individual. Joseph J. Egan argues that the "spiritually diseased and deteriorated condition" of the " 'white' Anglo-American community" is being "wryly, pathetically reflected in the 'ghostly white' color . . . of the 'leper' it abhors,"[7] but in fact Cable's attitude toward the American and Creole worlds he depicts is (characteristically) more ambivalent than Egan's remarks would suggest. Cable admires Poquelin, but makes it clear that the Creole's fortune was made by smuggling and slave trading, two activities that Cable personally abhorred and that were curtailed with the advent of the Yankee government. It is no pun to say that Cable refused to see his world in black and white terms; and the deliberate blurring of the identities of "Little White," of the bronzed and dark eyed Poquelin, and of the dark-turned-white Jacques suggests this. In fact, the blurring of seemingly antithetical characters was a device used with great effectiveness in *The Grandissimes* where, for example, Agricola and Bras-Coupé constitute a "highly ironic pairing of doubles"; they—like Little White and *les frères Poquelin*— prove to be "brothers . . . in the larger sense that all men are brothers."[8]

Cable's remarkable handling of the character of Little White underscores his theme that matters are not always as they appear. That the community fails to comprehend this truism reaches a climax in the shivaree scene, in which an unruly mob attempts to force Poquelin to interact with them. The shivaree scene is especially noteworthy, however, in that it brings forth the author's extraordinarily subtle sense of humor, which usually takes the form of irony. Most readers, of course, would never think of regarding "Jean-ah Poquelin" as humorous; indeed, Louis D. Rubin, Jr. has characterized it as being "perhaps the most somber of all the stories of *Old Creole Days*."[9] Even so, it is striated with the distinctively Cablesque humor that Michael L. Campbell aptly characterizes as "a pervasive irony that goes beyond mere verbal trickery to express a deep sense of anger and frustration over the human capacity for narrow caste pride, injustice, and mindless cruelty . . ."[10] Campbell's observation, although made specifically in reference to *The Grandissimes,* applies equally well to "Jean-ah Poquelin," and especially the shivaree scene. It opens with White and his wife Patty sitting on their doorstep, watching the blatantly symbolic setting sun. Little White fears that Poquelin might be " 'concocting some mischief' " (201), although in fact the old man is dying while the rest of the community—Americans and Creoles alike—really are "concocting some mischief": a cruel shivaree. The theme of appearances versus reality is reiterated in Patty's distress over the vision of the moon seeming to climb down one of the chimneys of the Poquelin mansion, and she attempts to dissuade White from confronting the shivaree mob. That the shivaree will be as cruel as she fears is signified by Cable's brief report of the event's inception: " '. . . Why don't you shivaree him?' Felicitous suggestion" (201). The curt, sarcastic appraisal—"Felicitous suggestion"—utilizes precisely the sort of sophisticated diction that would not be comprehended by the mob itself, and it is as eloquent in its two words as was the opening paragraph with its 118 words. Cable similarly presents irony via style in his description of the shivaree as it is first perceived by the Whites: "Down the street arose a great hubbub. Dogs and boys were howling and barking. . . ."(203) The syntax of the second sentence is intentionally fractured. By using a double subject and double predicate, Cable states that "boys" were "barking." This dehumanization process, the reduction of the shivaree's participants to animals, is continued in the observation that they were "clanking cow-bells" and "whinnying" (203). As he intercepts the mob (Cable intrudes into his text to note that his pen "hesitates on the word" [203]), White picks out its leader on the basis of "the size and clatter of his tin pan," bulk and noisiness generally being associated with the "leaders" of herds of elephants and cattle, not people. This leader (whose surname, Bienvenu, ironically means "Welcome") announces that White and Poquelin (not himself) are drunk and that the mob's purpose in visiting Poquelin is to ask for a $250 contribution to a local charity hospital—not realizing, of course, that Poquelin's entire house is a virtual hospital and that he is motivated to lead a reclusive life out of charity for his brother. Cable suddenly drops his blatant humor—but retains the subtler irony of situation—as the story draws to its unforgettable close. The mob, temporarily distracted by their shivaree of an old Dutchwoman, returns to Poquelin's house only to find themselves as the mourners at the old man's makeshift funeral—a role usually reserved, ironically enough, for the friends and family of the deceased. With White providing the eulogy, the patently humane African mute, "with the strength of an ape" (209), carried Poquelin's coffin into the swamplands so insistently associated with him; while "little Jacques" (or, more precisely, his "living remains" [209]) goes with the mute to find a new home in the leper colony—a home surely far worse than the "haunted house" in which he had remained hidden for the previous seven years.

The seemingly "haunted" house, the mysterious concealed loved one, the often cruel curiosity of townspeople—all are features arguing that "Jean-ah Poquelin" was written in the venerable tradition of Southern Gothic fiction; and in fact its affinities with such stories as "The Fall of the House of Usher" and "A Rose for Emily"—one might add *To Kill a Mockingbird,* with the mystery of Boo Radley—are well documented.[11] But it would be atypical of Cable to write a story in the popular Gothic mode as an end in itself. "Jean-ah Poquelin" is foremost a tale of brotherly love; far from being the Cain figure presumed by the townspeople (183), Poquelin is literally his "brother's keeper" (Gen. 8.9), even willing to share fully in the exclusion from community life that since biblical times has been the sorry lot of the leper.[12] It is a tale of Christian tolerance, of courage in the face of isolation and intimidation, and of endurance despite personal and communal turmoil. Jean-ah Poquelin, Little White, and the African mute may be seen as members of that select group of Cable characters—Posson Jone', Jules St.-Ange, Madame Delphine, Madame John—who are "true Christians" despite their human limitations and their dubious status in society. Like Flannery O'Connor seventy-five years later, Cable managed to steer clear of hagiography while creating a spiritually inspiring story that is also dramatically engrossing and artistically wrought. Small wonder that Fred Lewis Pattee termed "Jean-ah Poquelin" among the most perfect of American short stories.[13]

The Taint of Caste:
" 'Tite Poulette"

S ANDWICHED between two of the masterpieces of *Old Creole Days*,
"Jean-ah Poquelin" and "'Sieur George," is " 'Tite Poulette," the product of Cable's research in the municipal archives and newspapers of old New
Orleans,[1] and probably one of the earliest short stories he wrote.[2] It is
perhaps because of these factors that " 'Tite Poulette" is the most unevenly
rewarding of the eight tales in the collection. In some respects, such as the
handling of the story's opening and the use of the blurred identity motif,
" 'Tite Poulette" shows Cable at his best, in masterful control of his material
and writing with the textual and emotional density that is a hallmark of his
finest fiction. In other respects, including narrative technique, Cable seems
to be a more hesitant writer, apparently unable either to judge when the
reader will be confused by a particular element, or to edit the ineffective use
of a fundamentally sound technique. And in still other respects, most
noticeably the story's ending, " 'Tite Poulette" displays several of the weaknesses that were to plague Cable throughout his career as a writer. In the
final analysis, it is to Cable's credit as a literary artist that despite its myriad
flaws, " 'Tite Poulette" proves to be a moving and readable tale.

As is customary with Cable's fiction, the opening paragraph is vital for an
understanding of the story's plot, characters, themes, and motifs:

> Kristian Koppig was a rosy-faced, beardless young Dutchman. He was
> one of that army of gentlemen who, after the purchase of Louisiana,
> swarmed from all parts of the commercial world, over the mountains of
> Franco-Spanish exclusiveness, like the Goths over the Pyrenees, and
> settled down in New Orleans to pick up their fortunes, with the diligence
> of hungry pigeons. He may have been a German; the distinction was too
> fine for Creole haste and disrelish. (213)

As is borne out by the rest of the story, virtually everything the reader needs
to know about Koppig is presented in the first sentence: "Kristian Koppig
was a rosy-faced, beardless young Dutchman." That his face is "rosy"

suggests his freshness, youth, and innocence—qualities that are effectively reiterated in the adjectives "beardless" and "young," and that render him something of a helpless innocent when confronted with the complexity and dubious morality of a society locked in a racial caste system. Further, he is a "Dutchman"; that oft-repeated fact, coupled with the foreign look and sound of the name "Kristian Koppig," underscore his status as what I have identified elsewhere as an "interloper."[3] Linguistically, culturally, and socially, Koppig is in an insistently alien environment, a situation that helps make plausible his persistent faux pas and his misinterpretations of experience, while it simultaneously ensures that he observes—and evaluates—the New Orleans social structure with an unusual degree of objectivity. This latter element stands in stark contrast to the final statement of the paragraph: "He may have been a German; the distinction was too fine for Creole haste and disrelish." In one sentence, Cable has introduced several of the most important themes and motifs of the story. First, that Koppig has been assigned the label of "Dutchman" even though he may have been a German [Deutsch] suggests the most salient features of social classifications in New Orleans: these classifications are made with "haste"; they reflect "disrelish"; and, being based upon superficial factors, they are made without regard for the individual involved. The arbitrariness, power, and pervasiveness of the New Orleans caste system are such that even a foreigner is immediately assigned a position (accurate or otherwise) within it, and is treated accordingly. What more eloquent statement of the cruelty and injustice of the social system than that (with the notable exceptions of Madame John and her daughter) Koppig is automatically scorned and brutalized by the locals simply because he is "Dutch"—a situation that is particularly shocking in that this blue-eyed foreigner with his blatantly Nordic features could not possibly be anything but a pure Caucasian. In effect, what little information we receive of the New Orleans social structure in this opening paragraph is vital for our understanding of the perpetual stress and fear experienced by Madame John and her white (albeit legally black) daughter, 'Tite Poulette. Closely aligned with this, the confusion over Koppig's nationality introduces the twin motifs of unclear identity and concealment versus revelation, matters to be examined at some length below.

The initial paragraph also introduces several elements that Cable handles with varying degrees of success in the course of the story. First, there is the issue of money. The references to the "purchase" (not "acquisition") of Louisiana, to the "commercial world," and to the nonnatives who "swarmed" to New Orleans "to pick up their fortunes" suggest the mercenary attitude that was responsible for the establishment of the slave system in the first place, and that for centuries thereafter continued to render viable the patently unjust system of "legal" racial type. But although in " 'Tite Poulette" Cable had intended to explore the complex relationship between money, sex, and race, he unfortunately presents this triad with less than optimum effectiveness.

Before leaving this consideration of the story's opening paragraph, we must consider two more elements. First, the reference to the hungry pigeons introduces the bird imagery that constitutes a minor, but nevertheless striking, feature of the story. 'Tite Poulette (literally "little chick" [221]) is, for example, commonly associated with the mockingbird (e.g., 215); and according to Southern folk belief, it is a sin to injure this most beautiful and harmless of God's creatures. Also, the first paragraph offers a glimmer of the author's characteristic fondness for playing with words: the "gentlemen" who are mentioned at the beginning of the second sentence are quickly reduced to "Goths." The simile not only suggests the vast numbers and coarse materialism of the foreigners who invaded New Orleans, but it also suggests that those who present themselves as "gentlemen" may be something vastly different—an aspect of the unclear identities theme that is best dramatized in this story by Monsieur de la Rue, the smooth-talking villain who is never without his deadly "sword cane."

The second paragraph of the story's opening is similarly vital for the introduction of themes and motifs:

> [Koppig] made his home in a room with one dormer window looking out, and somewhat down, upon a building opposite, which still stands, flush with the street, a century old. Its big, round-arched windows in a long, second-story row, are walled up, and two or three from time to time have had smaller windows let into them again, with odd little latticed peep-holes in their batten shutters. This had already been done when Kristian Koppig first began to look at them from his solitary dormer window. (213)[4]

Cable's penchant for utilizing homes in the presentation of character and situation is quite apparent in this paragraph. Koppig, whose ignorance of New Orleans life and general naiveté become obvious in the course of the story, lives in just one room—an apt emblem of his limited experience. But Cable reiterates throughout the story that the room does have a window through which Koppig is able to observe the world of New Orleans, and that he is able to utilize almost as a visual bridge between himself and the otherwise inaccessible 'Tite Poulette. Further, that the window "look[s] out, and somewhat down," upon the building across the street creates the impression that Koppig is situated like a member of an audience in a balcony observing a play. That impression is in keeping with the theatrical quality of the story; but it also may call to mind a young man in a situation similar to that of Koppig—Giovanni Guasconti of Hawthorne's "Rappaccini's Daughter" (1844). As a native of southern Italy, Guasconti is an alien in Padua, and his ignorance is responsible for his being drawn into an unfortunate alliance with the beautiful girl he observes from his apartment window. It would be unwise to make too much of the similarities between " 'Tite Poulette" and "Rappaccini's Daughter"; indeed, the seriocomic interlude involving 'Tite Poulette's well-intended drowning of her "wretched little botanical specimens" in cigar boxes on the windowsill (226) may have been intended humorously to undercut any attempts to compare the two tales. But the fact remains that Cable does share with Hawthorne an awareness of the fictional possibilities of houses and windows. This awareness comes into full play when Cable describes the residence of Madame John and her daughter. The building features large windows that have been "walled up"; however, "two or three from time to time have had smaller windows let into them again, with odd little latticed peep-holes in their batten shutters." In effect, the building itself reflects the situation of Madame John and her daughter. As much as possible, they have attempted to barricade themselves away from a world that has been a source of misery to Madame John ("something told you, as you looked at her, that she was one who had had to learn a great deal in this troublesome life" [214]) and that promises to treat her beautiful young daughter in no better fashion. Indeed, the simple fact that the building in which they live had previously been an army barracks (213) underscores the two women's determination to defend themselves against the hostile world. But as the peepholes suggest, it is simply not practical to cut oneself off entirely from the world; desperately in need of funds, Madame John must literally wear another type of peephole—the satin mask of a paid dancer at the notorious Salle de Condé. And in addition to serving as symbols of Madame John's changing relationship with the outside world, the peepholes are ideal emblems for three of the commonest motifs in Cable's fiction: benevolent voyeurism, unclear identity, and concealment versus revelation.

The motif of benevolent voyeurism is handled in a remarkably complex fashion. Voyeurism in Cable generally is devoid of its usual associations of depravity or the sinister; his voyeur is typically a man who watches over a helpless female so as to be ready to aid her in the event of a crisis. Essentially, this is the role assumed by Koppig. His voyeurism begins innocently enough: Koppig "noticed" (218) the arrival of the villainous Monsieur de la Rue at the home of Madame John across the street. Being instinctively protective—albeit a "trifle dull" (219)—Koppig observes the old barracks on Sunday (when Monsieur de la Rue's Salle de Condé is open) to see if 'Tite Poulette will emerge to go to work: "The young man watched the opposite window steadily and painfully from early in the afternoon until the moon shone bright; and from the time the moon shone bright until Madame John . . . stepped through the wicket . . . and hurried off toward the *Rue Condé*" (219–20). Ostensibly Koppig is relieved that it is only the mother who must resort to professional dancing, and his mind, "glad to return to its own

unimpassioned affairs, relapsed into quietude" (220); but the very fact that
he felt so protective about 'Tite Poulette should have indicated to him—as it
does to the reader—that he has embryonic romantic feelings for the young
girl. The emergence of those feelings is signified by qualitative changes in
Koppig's voyeurism. What began as a simple glance at Monsieur de la Rue's
arrival becomes automatic and unconscious: Koppig "never notic[ed]" that
at night he "staid at home with his window darkened" so he could watch
'Tite Poulette (220). After Koppig is laid off from his job as a clerk,
voyeurism becomes a more conscious feature of his domestic routine, and
he spends his afternoons "at his dormer window reading and glancing down
at the little casement opposite" (226). Ultimately his voyeurism overtly
reflects his defensiveness of 'Tite Poulette. As Monsieur de la Rue arrives for
a confrontation with the two women, Koppig "stood up at the window [,]
prepared to become a bold spectator of what might follow" (227). And
much as Cable's treatment of voyeurism is sufficiently flexible at this early
stage of his career to permit it to serve as the gauge of Koppig's growing
feelings for 'Tite Poulette, so too he has spared Koppig the usual fate of his
voyeurs: far from being the helpless observer of a tragedy, Koppig actively
involves himself in the personal affairs of the two women, and although he
is stabbed for his troubles, ultimately he manages to foster a happy resolution to the story's woes. Cable has further demonstrated the flexibility of
this early voyeurism by making it two-way: the women begin to steal
glances at Koppig (e.g., 223–24), and in the story's climactic scene, Madame
John "gazed upon the pair, undiscovered" (242) as Koppig declares his love
for 'Tite Poulette. Even in this early story, then, Cable is taking advantage
of the rich technical possibilities offered by the motif of benevolent voyeurism.

Comparable skill is revealed by Cable's handling of the matter of unclear
identity. There is of course the confusion over Koppig's nationality (in fact,
he is a Hollander [223]), but unclear identities are most apparent in the broad
areas of personal names and racial types. For example, we never learn the
true name of Madame John (sometimes called "Zalli"). Cable, with characteristic coyness, refers to her as a woman "by the name—or going by the
name—of Madame John" (214); only a page later, he explains that a "gay
gentleman" named John used to live nearby, and "As his parents lived with
him, his wife would, according to custom, have been called Madame John;
but he had no wife" (215–16). Thus at the same time that Cable implies that
Zalli was married to John (she even wears "widow's weeds" after his death
[216]), he suggests that they saw one another only at quadroon balls (217).
The confusion over Zalli's personal name and marital status is intentionally
never resolved, and it serves as Cable's eloquent statement about the social,
psychological, and legal limbo occupied by quadroon women. This limbo is
made all the more nightmarish by the fact that "You would hardly have

thought of her being 'colored' "; Cable is careful to note that she is a "palish handsome woman" with "nearly straight hair" (214). His only overt reference to her black ancestry is that she has "that vivid black eye so peculiar to her kind" (214). Cable's transparent point is that, except for her eyes, Madame John looks Caucasian. That she is a quadroon (and therefore legally black) is clearly an arbitrary legal formality. So to underscore the arbitrariness of her official status as a nonwhite, Cable takes care to downplay Zalli's appearance. After mentioning its most salient features, he concentrates on what really identifies her as a quadroon—her situation. It is her shame at having to dance at the Salle de Condé, plus her palpable fear of the power of Monsieur de la Rue, that signify that legally and socially—even if not physically—she is a "woman of color." This confusion over identity is even more extreme in the case of 'Tite Poulette. We never learn her real name. Madame John refers to her occasionally as 'Tite Poulette, but more often the girl is spoken of as her "daughter." Yet even this seemingly incontrovertible element of identity is assailed: if Madame John is truly her mother, then who—biologically or legally—is her father? Monsieur John? Or another customer at the quadroon balls? And if indeed Madame John is telling the truth at the story's climax that 'Tite Poulette is the daughter of a Spanish couple who died of yellow fever, then who were these people, and what is 'Tite Poulette's Christian name? But the deliberate confusion over the girl's name, parentage, and nationality is relatively minor compared with the confusion over her racial identity. As with her mother (real or adoptive) Madame John, 'Tite Poulette is legally black and, as such, prey to the libidinous Monsieur de la Rue. But as the street lads have noted, she is " 'white like a water lily! White—like a magnolia!' " (214), and Koppig himself points out that " 'if she were in Holland today, not one of a hundred suitors would detect the hidden blemish' " (223). The topper, of course, comes at the climax of the story. Quickly producing some "sworn papers" (243), Madame John declares that 'Tite Poulette's parents were Spanish—and instantly a legal black becomes a legal Caucasian, with all rights and privileges appertaining thereto. Clearly Cable shares with William Faulkner a bitter appreciation of the power of legal documents to dictate one's race—and hence one's life. And however much this apparently contrived resolution to Cable's story smacks of deus ex machina, it is nonetheless chillingly appropriate in its implied but powerful condemnation of the arbitrariness of laws involving racial type.

A third (and closely related) motif that Cable handles with striking skill in " 'Tite Poulette" is the matter of concealment versus revelation. The most dramatic instance in the story of concealment followed by revelation is Zalli's declaration of the true parentage of 'Tite Poulette; however, even that disclosure seems to be concealing a great deal (one basic question: Were those "sworn papers" legitimate?). In fact, Cable throughout the story seems to prefer concealment *without* revelation. In addition to the unclear identities previously discussed, Cable presents this motif essentially through two devices: physical objects, and unfinished (or unclear) conversations. The physical objects pertaining to concealment include peepholes and personal attire. The peepholes in Zalli's home betoken a desire to cut oneself off from the world while acknowledging the sometimes unhappy necessity of interacting with it; but they also betoken the impulse to conceal unpleasant realities. In the case of Madame John, those realities are bitter; between her unclear relationship with Monsieur John, her grueling careers as a paid dancer and yellow fever nurse, and her anguish over 'Tite Poulette, she understandably seeks to conceal her unhappy past and her vulnerable daughter in the barracks where they live. Her attire is likewise designed for concealment. When she leaves her home to work at the Salle de Condé, Madame John is "much dressed and well muffled" (219); at the quadroon ball, it is customary to disguise oneself with a satin mask (217) and "a touch here and there of paint and powder" (220). Even such minor details as Monsieur de la Rue's cane (which conceals a rapier) and the very fact that Koppig gets his information about the neighborhood from a maker of wigs (215) suggest the society's basic impulse to use attire to conceal or deny the truth.

An even more dramatic illustration of the impulse to conceal is evident in Cable's reliance upon unfinished or unclear conversations. A striking example of this is the response of the wigmaker to Koppig's inquiry about Zalli:

> And who was this Madame John?
> "Why, you know!—she was"—said the wig-maker at the corner to Kristian Koppig—"I'll tell you. You know?—she was"—and the rest atomized off in a rasping whisper. She was the best yellow-fever nurse in a thousand yards around; but that is not what the wig-maker said. (215)

The whispering is indicative of the undercurrent of illicit sexuality in the story (Cable apparently is counting on his reader's awareness of the sexual implications of a woman's status as a quadroon, as well as of the notoriety of quadroon balls);[5] more cogently, the whispering is symptomatic of the concealment, rumors, half-truths, and defamation that are the consequences of a society's being structured around dubious racial and social distinctions. Similarly provocative is the unclear conversation between Madame John and Monsieur de la Rue in the local cathedral:

> "Madame John," whispered the manager.
> She courtesied.
> "Madame John, that young lady—is she your daughter?"
> "She—she—is my daughter," said Zalli, with somewhat of alarm in her face, *which the manager misinterpreted.*

"I think not, Madame John." He shook his head, *smiling as one too wise to be fooled.*

"Yes, Monsieur, she is my daughter."

"O no, Madame John, *it is only make-believe, I think.*"

"I swear she is, Monsieur de la Rue."

"Is that possible?" *pretending to waver,* but convinced in his heart of hearts, by Zalli's alarm, that she was lying. "But how? Why does she not come to our ball-room with you?"

Zalli, trying to get away from him, shrugged and smiled. "Each to his taste, Monsieur; it pleases her not." (224–25, emphasis mine)

Neither Madame John nor the reader can be sure what Monsieur de la Rue knows—or only pretends to know—of the parentage of 'Tite Poulette. The confusion, pretense, and cruelty that are so palpable in the exchange between Madame John and her employer convey perfectly the perpetual stress and uncertainty to be endured by a quadroon living in what Koppig terms "'this wicked city'" (222). Unfortunately, Cable does not always use the technique of unfinished or unclear conversations to maximum advantage. It is one of a series of fictional elements that were not utilized with optimum effectiveness in this early story, including narrative technique, the presentation of sensitive issues, and characterization.

In "'Tite Poulette" Cable employs his customary semiomniscient, ironic narrator. Typical of the narrator's remarks is the following comment on the converted Spanish Barracks where Madame John and her daughter had lived when the story took place (i.e., in 1810):[6]

I do not know who lives there now. You might stand about on the opposite *banquette* for weeks and never find out. I suppose it is a residence, for it does not look like one. That is the rule in that region. (214)

The admitted ignorance of the narrator and the slightly flippant, almost sardonic tone of the passage are perfect for a story in which concealment and bitterness are so pervasive. But however well suited the semiomniscient narrator is for this particular story, the technique is not always handled well. Too often what is meant to be ironic or whimsical proves to be rather annoying, as in the following passage:

"But the woman certainly will not attempt"—said [Koppig] to himself—"no, no! she cannot." Not being able to guess what he meant, I cannot say whether she could or not. (219)

What was designed to illustrate Koppig's often-mentioned "dullness" seems instead to be part of an unfortunate pattern in "'Tite Poulette": passages that seem to reflect less the admitted ignorance of a semiomniscient narrator than the hesitation of an author unsure of what to say (or how to say it).

Granted, in a few instances the lack of clarity seems intentional, and is apparently a reflection of Cable's love of wordplay and whimsy. Such is the case in the following passage from the story's second paragraph: "This had already been done when Kristian Koppig first began to look at them from his solitary dormer window" (213). It is clear from the context that "This" refers to the installation of peepholes in the blocked windows, but the word "them" has several possible antecedents: it could refer to the "big, round-arched windows"; to the "smaller windows" that were "let into them"; to the "little latticed peep-holes"; or to the "batten shutters." A case could be made for each of these possible antecedents, but even so, "them" seems to refer to Madame John and 'Tite Poulette—neither of whom has been mentioned at this point in the story. In this particular instance, the uncertainty about the word "them" seems deliberate; in part, it constitutes foreshadowing. Too often, however, the unclear passages do not seem to have been intentional; and although in most cases these passages are brief, their brevity does not mitigate the problems they create. For example: "Kristian Koppig shut his window. Nothing but a generous heart and a Dutchman's phlegm could have done so at the moment. And even thou, Kristian Koppig!—for the window closed very slowly" (222). Even in its context, this passage makes little sense. The reader might be able to accept this obscure passage if it were presented by the semiomniscient narrator, but unfortunately it is too obviously a simple example of shaky writing. In fact, so often is Cable's presence evident (if unwittingly) in the story—and so often does the narrator seem to disappear—that at times it is momentarily confusing to find the narrator (or is it Cable?) referring to himself in the first person. The difficulties with the semiomniscient narrator are compounded by the fact that the story is generally told from the point of view of Koppig. Much of the emotional impact of the story is the result of the ignorant foreigner's attempts to fathom the complex social structure of New Orleans, and Cable takes advantage of this by having Koppig write to his mother in Holland about his experiences and observations:

> "In this wicked city, I see none so fair as the poor girl who lives opposite me, and who, alas! though so fair, is one of those whom the taint of caste has cursed. She lives a lonely, innocent life in the midst of corruption, like the lilies I find here in the marshes, and I have great pity for her. 'God defend her,' I said to-night to a fellow clerk, 'I see no help for her.' I know there is a natural, and I think proper, horror of mixed blood (excuse the mention, sweet mother), and I feel it, too; and yet if she were in Holland to-day, not one of a hundred suitors would detect the hidden blemish." (222–23)

The letter offers insights into Koppig's character (he pities 'Tite Poulette, but also feels disgust for the miscegenation that produced her); at the same time, the letter enables Koppig to criticize the cruel racial caste system with a directness not granted the narrator. Clearly the epistolary interludes are an ideal form of narrative technique for this particular story, but unfortunately Cable includes the fragments of only two of Koppig's letters to his mother. The story would have gained tremendous impact had it been told primarily in the form of letters; but Cable—apparently seeking to avoid the admittedly limited (and hence potentially distorting) first-person narration offered by epistolary fiction—opted instead to try to combine the single point of view of Koppig with the broader knowledge of the semiomniscient narrator. There is nothing inherently wrong with this, but the results are sometimes confusing:

> One night, on the mother's return [from the Salle de Condé], Kristian Koppig coming to his room nearly at the same moment, there was much earnest conversation, *which he could see, but not hear.*
> " 'Tite Poulette," said Madame John, "you are seventeen."
> "True, Maman."
> "Ah! my child, I see not how you are to meet the future."
> . . . .
> "[Y]ou will be lonely, lonely, all your poor life long. There is no place in this world for us poor women. I wish that we were either white or black!"—and the tears, two "shining ones," stood in the poor quadroon's eyes.
> The daughter stood up, her eyes flashing. (220–21, emphasis mine)

Recognizing the need to provide the reader with fuller information about the suffering of Madame John and 'Tite Poulette, Cable rather awkwardly reports a conversation that Koppig sees but cannot hear; and he further compounds the problem by mentioning elements that even Koppig could not have seen from his vantage point across the street—the mother's tears, and the daughter's flashing eyes. A similar but far more effective scene occurs eight pages later. Koppig, rushing to the street door to avert possible trouble between Monsieur de la Rue and Madame John, observes their encounter:

> Inside could just be descried Madame John. The manager bowed, smiled, talked, talked on, held money in his hand, bowed, smiled, talked on, flourished the money, smiled, bowed, talked on and plainly persisted in some intention to which Madame John was steadfastly opposed.
> The window above, too,—it was Kristian Koppig who noticed that,— opened a wee bit, like the shell of a terrapin. Presently the manager lifted his foot and put forward an arm, as though he would enter the gate by pushing, but as quick as gunpowder it clapped—in his face! (229)

The passage is powerful precisely because Cable maintains Koppig's limited point of view. The lack of dialogue, far from being a liability, enhances our

awareness of the intense emotions of the encounter, as well as the help-
lessness of Koppig in his status as an observer. Cable is skillfully utilizing
one of the most basic of narrative techniques, the dumb show; and although
at times the device seems melodramatic and posed—"Ah, how she wept!
Sob, sob, sob; gasps and sighs and stifled ejaculations, her small right hand
clinched and beating on her mother's knee; and the mother weeping over
her" (222)—the fact remains that Cable does use theatrical devices to good
advantage in "'Tite Poulette." This theatricality is particularly evident in his
reliance upon sound and movement in the presentation of key scenes. In the
following passage, the word "That!" signifies a knife wound:

> "That!" and "That!" and "That!" and the poor Dutchman struck wildly
> here and there, grasped the air, shut his eyes, staggered, reeled, fell, rose
> half up, fell again for good, and they were kicking him and jumping on
> him. All at once they scampered. Zalli had found the night-watch.
> "Buz-z-z-z!" went a rattle. "Buz-z-z-z!" went another.
> "Pick him up."
> "Is he alive?"
> "Can't tell; hold him steady; lead the way, misses."
> "He's bleeding all over my breeches."
> "This way—here—around this corner."
> "This way now—only two squares more."
> "Here we are."
> "Rap-rap-rap!" on the old brass knocker. Curses on the narrow wicket,
> more on the dark archway, more still on the winding stairs.
> Up at last and into the room. (236–37)

The run-on quality of the first sentence, the sheer number of verbs included, and the fact that Cable alternates monosyllabic words ("fell") and
verb phrases ("rose half up") convey as vividly as stage directions the
awkward movement and disorientation of the stabbed Koppig. Likewise,
the rather disjointed dialogue between the participants ("Pick him up." "Is
he alive?") and the uncertainty over who is actually speaking (thanks to the
Hemingwayesque lack of speech tags) underscore the confusion and con-
tribute to the pace of the passage, while simultaneously suggesting movement ("This way—here—around this corner"). Some of the most powerful
passages in "'Tite Poulette" reflect Cable's awareness of the possibilities of
theatrical devices to enhance narration; but instead of incorporating these
devices more fully, he seems to draw back from them. Immediately following the scene just discussed, Cable lapses into what is apparently his own
voice:

> And there lies the young Dutch neighbor . . . O, Woman!—that knows
> no enemy so terrible as man! Come nigh, poor Woman, you have nothing
> to fear. Lay your strange, electric touch upon the chilly flesh; it strikes no
> eager mischief along the fainting veins. (237)

And so on, for a fairly long paragraph. In abandoning the powerful technique of dramatization, Cable self-consciously overwrites, and the resultant purple prose weakens the story significantly.

The unevenness in the quality of the narration of " 'Tite Poulette"—Cable's apparent hesitation as to how best to present his material—has a counterpart in his seeming uncertainty over *what* to present. Specifically, Cable appears unsure about how much to explore the sensitive issues of religion, money, and sexuality—all of which are vitally concerned with the story's key issue, racial discrimination.

Unlike "Belles Demoiselles Plantation," " 'Tite Poulette" never approaches the level of religious allegory, but nonetheless religion does occupy a significant—if not entirely clear—position in the story. It is no accident that Koppig's given name is "Kristian"; as the Dutchman gradually progresses from innocence to experience in the alien land, the story does assume a slightly fantastic Bunyanesque atmosphere, and Koppig generally fulfills the expectations aroused by his given name. Kindly, well meaning, and protective, Koppig is an almost ideal rendering of the modern man of God, and his Christian dimension is further underscored by his attendance at church,[7] his being the passive victim of violence, and his abhorrence of the Salle de Condé, which features performances on "the Sabbath" (219). But at the same time that Cable posits Koppig as a sterling Christian, he portrays him as a "dolt" (234). The ploy offers considerable comic relief to this grim story, as we watch Koppig commit sundry social blunders and toil over writing simple notes ("Two hours slipped by. He made a new pen, washed and refilled his inkstand, mended his 'abominable!' chair, and after two hours more made another attempt, and another failure. 'My head aches,' said he, and lay down on his couch . . ." [231]). And more importantly, Koppig's dull-wittedness rescues him from the one-dimensionality of allegorical characterization, while rendering somewhat more plausible his impulse to become involved in the personal lives of his neighbors. But by pushing provinciality virtually to clownishness, Cable fails to guide his reader's reaction to the protagonist's spiritual dimension (Is Koppig kind because he is a Christian, or because he is a fool?) and, concomitantly, to the broader Christian foundation of " 'Tite Poulette." We can never be sure how to react to the story's many references to religion. For example, when the doctor attending the wounded Koppig tells Madame John that " 'They are thanking you in heaven' " for having raised 'Tite Poulette (240), the reader is inclined to take the comment positively—but perhaps not, if he bears in mind Koppig's twofold status as Christian and dolt, or the palpable irony of an earlier remark that Zalli's beloved Monsieur John was "in heaven—so the priest said—" (218). More significantly, the lovely 'Tite Poulette would appear to be speaking for Cable when she, "with a gentle, but stately smile," asserts that " 'God made us. He made us just as we are; not more white, not more black' " (221). But what seems to be a sensible plea for the acceptance of an unchangeable, God-directed situation is undercut when 'Tite Poulette learns that Caucasian men (whom legally she can never marry) find her attractive: "The daughter's face was thrown into the mother's lap, not so well satisfied, now, with God's handiwork" (222). The presentation of the incompatibility of bitter reality and the seemingly naive platitudes of religious teaching is, in itself, a statement about the challenges of following a Christian lifestyle in a world essentially devoid of faith. This is an extremely important statement that does much to illuminate Cable's attitude toward racial and social injustice, and the possibility of their resolution through organized religion; but unfortunately it is seriously obscured by the emphasis on Koppig's gaucherie and the heavy reliance on irony.

Much as the sensitive issue of religion is handled with less than optimum effectiveness in "'Tite Poulette," so too with the matter of money. The opening paragraphs of the tale subtly suggest the importance of money in nineteenth-century Louisiana, and in fact much of the plot revolves around the financial situation of Madame John. Her dying lover had left her his home, but "With the fatal caution which characterizes ignorance, she sold the property and placed the proceeds in a bank, which made haste to fail" (216). Left to her own resources, Madame John finds occasional employment as a yellow fever nurse and hairdresser, but she and her daughter "began to be in want" (218). This lack of marketable skills and the total ignorance of financial matters were elements that Cable would explore time and again in his fiction, most notably in his novel *Dr. Sevier* (1885). Far from being genteel or charming, the inability to deal effectively with the financial realities of the contemporary world left one the helpless victim of those who did have money and, consequently, power. In "'Tite Poulette," this situation is graphically depicted in Zalli's tense relationship with her employer, the reprehensible Monsieur de la Rue. Unable to find decent work, Madame John must perform in de la Rue's seamy Salle de Condé: "It had to be done. It brought some pay, and pay was bread" (220). By threatening to dismiss her and by forcing her to go to his office for her paycheck, Monsieur de la Rue exerts total control over Zalli's current life, her future, and her innocent daughter, whom he lusts after in true villainous fashion. Cable is illustrating the close relationship between financial security and sexual power: the rich dominate, and the poor are their victims. Cable also incorporates a third strand in this complex social pattern—race: " 'There is no place in this world for us poor women. I wish that we were either white or black!' " (221). Playing upon the double meaning of "poor" (poverty-stricken, and unfortunate), Cable is arguing in "'Tite Poulette" that poverty is the result of uncertain race—and uncertain race is the result of the sexual dominance of the rich (Caucasians) over the poor (legal blacks). The three interrelated factors of poverty, sexual victimization, and mixed blood constitute a vicious cycle that seems destined to continue indefinitely. One might wish that Cable had dealt with this complex sociological problem more fully in " 'Tite Poulette," but he seems to have recognized that it was too broad, too knotty, and too sensitive for the limited scope of the short story. He would examine it at great length in his masterpiece, *The Grandissimes* (1880).

It must be noted, however, that one element touched upon rather fully is sexuality, although Cable often brushes past the problem of victimization. In deference to the publishing standards of his day, Cable does not discuss sex overtly; but his oblique treatment of it—and in particular of illicit sex— proves in some respects to be quite bold. For example, part of what makes Zalli such an intriguing character is that Cable conveys a strong sense of her sexuality. The fact that she has assumed the title of "Madame John" and wears mourning—even though the late Monsieur John "had no wife" (216)—clearly indicates that she had been his mistress; and there is the distinct possibility that 'Tite Poulette is their illegitimate daughter. Indeed, the simple fact that Madame John has been a dancer at the quadroon balls— both years before, when they were relatively respectable, and in their later reprehensible form—imparts to her an aura of sensuous mystery that strik- ingly complements her strong maternal feelings for 'Tite Poulette. It is in keeping with Cable's sensuous portrait of Madame John that Koppig one day "happened to see, late in the afternoon,—hardly conscious that he was looking across the street,—that Madame John was—dressing" (232). The slight hesitation suggested by the dash before "dressing" is indicative of Koppig's dismay at her decision to continue dancing for de la Rue, while it also is designed to give the reader a little jolt such as Koppig received. Koppig clearly is responding to the sexuality of Madame John; significantly, he will not have a comparable response to 'Tite Poulette—ostensibly the object of his affections—until the end of the story. Part of what makes his belated physical response to the girl so peculiar is that he seems to be the only man in town who is not cognizant of her sexual potential. What Cable coyly terms "frantic lads" perpetually watch and comment on her (216), and Monsieur de la Rue sounds out Zalli about her after hotly pursuing the two women into church (224–25). But although Cable points up the girl's sexual potential, he is even more careful to emphasize her innocence. Those "frantic" youths treat her with total respect: "though theirs were only the loose New Orleans morals of over fifty years ago, their unleashed tongues never had attempted any greater liberty than to take up the pet name, 'Tite Poulette" (217). Further, even the dull-witted Koppig is struck by the fact that " 'She lives a lonely, innocent life in the midst of corruption, like the lilies I find here in the marshes' " (222). It is quite likely that Cable has in mind Shakespeare's Sonnet 94, line 14 ("Lilies that fester smell far worse than weeds"). 'Tite Poulette seems almost destined to lose her incredible innocence in this sexually charged, morally corrupt society, and it is a fate that Zalli and Koppig seek desperately to avert. Curiously, it is 'Tite Poulette's rather asexual innocence that heightens the emotional impact of the story's climactic scene, in which Koppig reveals his love for her both verbally and tactually. That scene begins with a one-sentence paragraph (its brevity and seeming isolation tend to rivet the reader's attention upon it), after the wounded Koppig has been carried to the home of Madame John:

So he lies—on 'Tite Poulette's own bed. (237)

In the purple passage that follows shortly thereafter (part of which was quoted above), the sexual undercurrent of the one-sentence paragraph is not mitigated by Cable's insistence upon the ailing Koppig's harmlessness to women:

Come nigh, poor Woman, you have nothing to fear. Lay your strange, electric touch upon the chilly flesh; it strikes no eager mischief along the fainting veins. Look your sweet looks upon the grimy face, and tenderly lay back the locks from the congested brows; no wicked misinterpretation lurks to bite your kindness. Be motherly, be sisterly, fear nought. Go, watch him by night; you may sleep at his feet and he will not stir. (237)

Cable then traces the way in which, as the months of convalescence roll by, Koppig's dormant sexuality begins to emerge. When he is "a man again" (241), he declares his love to 'Tite Poulette:

"God has made you very beautiful, 'Tite Poulette!"
She stirred not. He reached, and gently took her little hand, and as he drew her one step nearer, a tear fell from her long lashes. . . . The young man lifted the hand to lay it upon his lips, when, with a mild, firm force, it was drawn away, yet still rested in his own upon the bedside, like some weak thing snared, that could only not get free. . . .
"Thou wrong'st me, 'Tite Poulette. Thou dost not trust me; thou fearest the kiss may loosen the hands. But I tell thee nay. I have struggled hard, even to this hour, against Love, but I yield me now; I yield; I am his unconditioned prisoner forever. God forbid that I ask aught but that you will be my wife." (242)

The passage is noteworthy for several reasons. First, as Philip Butcher points out, Koppig's shift from "you" to "thou" serves to invite "comparison (already brought to mind by the interracial theme) with the Book of Ruth."[8] Further, although tame by modern standards, the scene is striking in that it touches upon what has heretofore not been acknowledged: the physical attraction between the two young people. Strangely enough for a love story, that attraction may strike the reader as being rather inappropriate, simply because of the situation and characters of Koppig and 'Tite Poulette. In terms of their situation, they really have had only slight, and generally negative, contact. Before Koppig's stabbing, their interaction consisted of an embarrassing accidental meeting (233–34), a report to 'Tite Poulette by Zalli that she had overheard Koppig commending the girl to God's protection (221–22), and some awkward eye contact: "The black eyes of the maiden and the blue over the way [i.e., of Koppig] . . . look[ed] into each other for the first time in life" (227). And after the stabbing, Koppig is evidently too weak and delirious to foster a meaningful relationship with anyone. Are we, then, to believe that their love is based essentially on two emotions: mutual pity (his for the daughter of a quadroon, hers for a wounded man) and mutual gratitude (his for the girl's medical attention, hers for the protection of a white man)? In short, except in the realm of sentimental fiction, their ostensible love really has no tenable basis in reality. This problem is further compounded by Cable's characterization of the two young people. 'Tite Poulette is depicted as an almost incredible model of purity; and Koppig, despite his physical bulk, is described as quiet (216), gentle (219), rosy (227), pretty (233), and, of course, "simple" and "slow-thinking" (220): in a word, bovine. He is fundamentally what Arlin Turner aptly terms "an awkward piece of stage furniture,"[9] and 'Tite Poulette, despite her prettiness and charm, has been romanticized to the point where she seems to be made of wax, totally lacking the flesh-and-blood credibility of her mother. For this odd couple to set romantic sparks flying is, one must admit, a bit unbelievable.

The difficulties with the characterizations of Koppig and 'Tite Poulette, and in particular with their alleged romance, are major factors contributing to the weak conclusion of the story. This is not to say that the conclusion is the weakest aspect of " 'Tite Poulette." That dubious distinction should go either to the lamentably overused eye imagery ("She whirled and attacked him with her eyes. 'Monsieur must not give himself the trouble!' she said, the eyes at the same time adding, 'Dare to come!' " [225]) or to the character of Monsieur de la Rue, so dastardly a stage villain that one half expects him to tie poor 'Tite Poulette to the nearest railroad track. But nonetheless, Madame John's revelation that 'Tite Poulette is Spanish, and therefore able to marry Koppig legally, does present serious problems. It is not that the reader is unprepared for the ending. Cable drops hints like stones that 'Tite Poulette looks incredibly Caucasian for someone with black ancestry; the Spanish couple who reportedly were her biological parents are mentioned a scant three pages before Zalli's declaration; and just before the announcement, Cable inserts a curious, hazy scene between Madame John and Koppig's attending physician in which she evidently admits to him, for no readily discernible reason, that she is not 'Tite Poulette's mother. It is to Cable's credit that he has Koppig declare his love for 'Tite Poulette before he learns she is white; but, then again, Koppig's well-documented dull-wittedness tends to undercut the impact of a Caucasian deciding to flaunt authority on behalf of a legal black (compare Huckleberry Finn's support of Jim: " 'All right, then, I'll *go* to hell" [chapter 31]). And the impact is further reduced when Madame John declares that 'Tite Poulette is in fact Caucasian. Far from being a situation of love conquering injustice, the union of Koppig and 'Tite Poulette will be tidy and legal; instead of sacrificing all for love, Koppig sacrifices nothing; or as Philip Butcher states the case, the ending "converts a piece of social criticism into an insipid fairy tale about a beautiful damsel whose right to marry the prince rests on the revelation that she is of royal birth, not on her human rights or personal worth."[10] Granted, Cable still is making his point about the arbitrariness of racial discrimination: all it takes is a sworn statement to transform a legal black into a " 'white as snow' " Caucasian (243). But, ironically, that point becomes lost in the reader's relief that Koppig will be able to marry 'Tite Poulette. In effect, by apparently glossing over racial discrimination with a "happy" twist ending, Cable seems to beg the issue around which the entire story was structured. Small wonder that the ending caused some consternation among Cable's readership. Charles DeKay, reviewing *Old Creole Days* in 1879, grumbled that the story "turns out rather tamely."[11] One dismayed quadroon reader wrote Cable to say that it would have been better if Madame John had lied about the girl's being Spanish—that, in fact, Madame John had denied her own maternity. A double twist ending, with Madame John admitting (even if only to the reader) that 'Tite Poulette really was her daughter—as is done in *Madame Delphine*—would have redoubled the impact of Cable's statement about the arbitrariness of racial classification, and it would have further illustrated Madame John's noble and self-sacrificing character. Indeed, one might argue that Cable was gravitating toward this in the conversation between Zalli and Koppig's doctor; it makes no sense for her to be telling him about 'Tite Poulette's "real" parents—and in particular within earshot of Koppig—unless she is planning to lie about 'Tite Poulette's birth. She seems to be using the doctor to test the community's probable reaction to her announcement of the adoption, and in fact the doctor doubts her: " 'I think perhaps, *perhaps* you are telling the truth' " (239). She then seems to back off from the story about the Spaniards, denying to Koppig that 'Tite Poulette was their child (but eventually, of course, insisting that she was). The curious scene with the doctor notwithstanding, there really is nothing in the story or in Cable's own remarks to suggest that Zalli lied about 'Tite Poulette's Spanish parents, and in fact the girl's being Caucasian spares Cable a sticky situation—how to handle the legality of her marriage with Koppig. A double twist ending would mean that the marriage was inter-racial, and therefore illegal. Cable, so enamored of marriage as a device for the resolution of plot difficulties, was not the sort of writer to entangle two sympathetic characters in such a complicated and painful situation. But Cable did acknowledge the point made by the quadroon reader, and just a few years later he would publish a more "truthful" reworking of the " 'Tite Poulette" story line: the novella *Madame Delphine*.

" 'Tite Poulette" occupies a unique position in Cable's fictional canon. It shows him honing (although with uneven results) his skills in areas such as narrative technique, while grappling with the most complex and sensitive issues of his day. " 'Tite Poulette" may not be a masterpiece, but it surely is a milestone in Cable's development as a literary artist.

Cable's Heart of Darkness:
" 'Sieur George"

IN 1923, Robert Underwood Johnson recalled in his *Remembered Yesterdays* how it was "a fresh and gentle southwest wind that blew into the office" of *Scribner's Monthly Magazine* in 1873 when there arrived the manuscript of " 'Sieur George," a tale by an obscure New Orleans clerk named George Washington Cable.[1] As the assistant editor at *Scribner's,* Johnson was in an ideal position to appraise the reaction of Richard Watson Gilder and company to the little story from Louisiana; but even so his appraisal seems only partly just. "Fresh" the story undoubtedly was. At a time when typical *Scribner's* fare included Hans Christian Andersen's "The Flea and the Professor," Mary L. Sherman's saccharine poem "My Valentine," J. T. Headley's paean to the wonders of Philadelphia, and G. F Comfort's belabored treatise entitled "Should the Study of the Modern Precede that of the Ancient Languages?,"[2] Cable's story must have seemed as original, as exotic, as the region where it takes place. In the early 1870s the North was, of course, experiencing a postwar fascination with the conquered South; and it was both to nurture and to capitalize on this fascination that Edward King, assisted by illustrator J. Wells Champney, had been commissioned by *Scribner's* to prepare a series of essays entitled "The Great South" (published between July 1873 and December 1874). Cable was "discovered" by King on his visit to Louisiana, and it was he who brought " 'Sieur George" to the attention of the *Scribner's* editors. The popular and critical response to Cable's first published story was most encouraging; it effectively launched a literary career that was to span some forty years, and helped to usher in a general appreciation for Southern literature that continues to this day.

So the "freshness" of Johnson's appraisal seems valid; but what of the "gentle" wind that " 'Sieur George" allegedly generated? Louis D. Rubin, Jr., justly finds Johnson's remark "almost comically inappropriate,"[3] for in fact " 'Sieur George" is an uncompromising psychological study of the title character's moral, emotional, and physical degeneration in an alien environment. Indeed, in many respects " 'Sieur George" anticipates by thirty years the deterioration of Kurtz in Joseph Conrad's "Heart of Darkness."

That " 'Sieur George" is a study of degeneration is signified by the very description of the building in which the title character resides:

> In the heart of New Orleans stands a large four-story brick building, that has so stood for about three-quarters of a century. Its rooms are rented to a class of persons occupying them simply for lack of activity to find better and cheaper quarters elsewhere. With its gray stucco peeling off in broad patches, it has a solemn look of gentility in rags, and stands, or, as it were, hangs, about the corner of two ancient streets, like a faded fop who pretends to be looking for employment. (247)

Note that the first six words of the story emphasize the locale. On the most basic level, this is an element that would have had a far greater impact on the readers of 1873 than it would on those of a century later, and in fact Cable underscored the unusual setting of his tale by providing " 'Sieur George" with a subtitle that has since been dropped: "A Story of New Orleans." But more important than indicating the setting, the first six words introduce the predominant leitmotif of the tale: closure. As shall be seen, Cable progressively narrows the focus of his story—from New Orleans, to "the heart" of the city, to a particular building, to a courtyard of that building, to a two-room apartment off that courtyard, and finally to a mysterious trunk inside that apartment. For now, though, it is sufficient to note that closure (which proves to mean radically different things to the Creoles and to 'Sieur George) is insisted upon at the outset of the story.

The building itself is carefully rendered. As a "large four-story brick building," it creates an initial impression of solidity and permanence. This is enhanced by the fact that it has been standing for "three-quarters of a century"—a more ponderous, more impressive phrase than "seventy-five years." But Cable immediately undercuts his initial rendering of a venerable, solid structure: "its gray stucco [is] peeling off in broad patches." The color gray denotes not only advanced age, but also haziness and uncertainty: "a gray area." And in fact, for all the details Cable so carefully provides about the building, we have little concrete knowledge about its residents, and in particular about 'Sieur George; and the more Cable "peels" away George's facade in the course of the story, the less we really know—or wish to know—about him. Also, the remark about the "broad patches" of peeling stucco imparts to the building the quality of "gentility in rags," a phrase that aptly characterizes 'Sieur George in his "newly-repaired overcoat" (257). Similarly, the comparison of the building to "a faded fop who pretends to be looking for employment" anticipates 'Sieur George's deterioration to the point where he "never sought employment" (258), preferring to live off the fortune of the unnamed "Mademoiselle" whose daughter he adopts. Further, the Dickensian personification of the inanimate building prepares the reader for the behavior of 'Sieur George, who is alternately intensely active and virtually catatonic—a phenomenon indicative of his moral imbalance. It is clear, then, that Cable's rendering of the building in the opening paragraph involves not only straightforward description of an actual edifice (it is so precise, in fact, that ten years after the story's publication, Lafcadio Hearn was able to locate the building and describe it for the *Century*),[4] but also the creation of atmosphere and the characterization of the tale's protagonist.

The story's second paragraph is no less dense and vital than the first:

> Under its main archway is a dingy apothecary-shop. On one street is the bazaar of a *modiste en robes et chapeaux* and other humble shops; on the other, the immense batten doors with gratings over the lintels, barred and bolted with masses of cobwebbed iron, like the door of a donjon, are overhung by a creaking sign (left by the sheriff), on which is faintly discernible the mention of wines and liquors. A peep through one of the shops reveals a square court within, hung with many lines of wet clothes, its sides hugged by rotten staircases that seem vainly to clamber out of the rubbish. (247)

As Cable steadily narrows the focus in his discussion of the building, he first attends to its most visible, public elements: the shops. Anticipating Frowenfeld's drugstore in *The Grandissimes* by some eight years, Cable refers initially to a "dingy apothecary-shop." Rather surprisingly, it does not figure again in the story, but the curious association of "dinginess" with healing nicely conveys the distinctive combination of depravity and nobility that renders 'Sieur George himself so fascinating. In like fashion, one finds in the building "the bazaar of a *modiste en robes et chapeaux*"; the exotic word "bazaar," coupled with the studied sophistication of the French passage, prove ironic when undercut with the phrase "and other humble shops." Once again, this pseudogentility anticipates 'Sieur George's situation as a dashing soldier whose private life is dedicated to drinking, gambling, and deceiving. In fact, 'Sieur George's drinking problem is anticipated in the reference to the bar. In keeping with the closure motif, its door—bolted, oxymoronically, "with masses of cobwebbed iron"—is likened to that of a "donjon," an element that anticipates 'Sieur George's personal entrapment in a life of moral laxity. The bar's sign is especially significant in that it introduces two more of the story's most important motifs: lethargy, and concealment (which is closely aligned with closure). Cable never speaks of words written on the sign. Rather, he notes that "the mention" of alcoholic beverages is "faintly discernible." It is as if the bar owner—or his animate sign—lacked the inclination to advertise the liquor overtly and aggressively; instead, it is simply mentioned. This quality of lethargy or haziness is likewise conveyed by "faintly discernible," a phrase that also suggests concealment. Lethargy and concealment are further seen in the remark that "A peep through one of the shops reveals a square court within, hung with many lines of wet clothes. . . ." With the notable exception of the exterior of the building, few things in this story are directly observed. "Peeping" and eavesdropping are de rigueur, and as a result very little is ever truly understood. In this regard, the wet laundry assumes special significance. It is in keeping with the closure motif that it can be seen only by a "peep" through a shop; but the enclosure is less for security than for the concealment of something private and unattractive. Also noteworthy is the fact that there is nothing to suggest that the laundry ever dries. Its apparently perpetual wetness may call to mind that brilliant rendering of a lethargic existence, Tennyson's "The Lotos-Eaters" (1832), set in "A land where all things always seemed the same" (line 24).[5] Further, as with 'Sieur George's depraved existence, it is doubtful that the laundry is ever really clean—especially since it is hanging in a busy courtyard, the sides of which are "hugged by rotten staircases that seem vainly trying to clamber out of the rubbish." It is in keeping with the Dickensian animation motif that only the staircases, not the people, wish to leave the area. As Cable observes in the story's second sentence, the inhabitants remain there "simply for lack of activity to find better and cheaper quarters elsewhere."

Part and parcel with the atmosphere of inertia and concealment that Cable is so carefully creating is the building's landlord, one "Kookoo." Only a boy when he inherited the property, he "has grown old and wrinkled and brown, a sort of periodically animate mummy, in the business" (248). His lethargy is especially evident in the fact that he "takes all suggestions of repairs as personal insults" (248), but there is one field of endeavor to which he devotes fully fifty years: the satisfaction of his curiosity about his tenant, 'Sieur George. Although Cable utilizes an omniscient, intrusive narrator, the story is in good measure the record of the often misguided thoughts, comments, and actions of the curious landlord.

Cable's introduction of Kookoo's tenant is deliberately vague and misleading. In folkloric terms, 'Sieur George is a "mysterious stranger." He is initially referred to elusively as "a certain old man" whose "name no one knew" (248), and our first impression of him is his coming home drunk—an event that is reenacted "every evening":

It was his wont to be seen taking a straight—too straight—course toward his home, never careening to right or left, but now forcing himself slowly forward, as though there were a high gale in front, and now scudding briskly ahead at a ridiculous little dog-trot, as if there were a tornado behind. He would go up the main staircase very carefully, sometimes stopping half-way up for thirty or forty minutes' doze, but getting to the landing eventually, and tramping into his room in the second story, with no little elation to find it still there. Were it not for these slight symptoms of potations, he was such a one as you would pick out of a thousand for a miser. A year or two ago he suddenly disappeared. (248–49)

Typical of Cable's style is the precise depiction of physical movement, as is the infusion of words that are simultaneously ironic and whimsical: 'Sieur George's collapse into an alcoholic stupor is characterized rather cozily as a "doze"; his drunken behavior is said to exhibit "slight symptoms of potations," an incongruous blending of sublime diction and ridiculous action that is reminiscent of the "faded fop" passage of the story's opening.

But what is particularly characteristic of Cable's style is his handling of time. We are told that 'Sieur George's carouses happened on a daily basis "for many years" (248); we are then told that "a year or two ago he suddenly disappeared" (249); immediately thereafter a new paragraph begins, "A great many years ago, when the old house was still new, a young man with no baggage save a small hair-trunk, came and took the room . . ." (249); later in the same paragraph we learn how "He supposed he might stay fifty days—and he staid fifty years and over" (249); the next paragraph begins "But when he had been here about a year . . ." (249); and the subsequent paragraphs contain vague temporal phrases such as "Afterward" (250), "from that time on" (249), and "Many seasons came and went" (250). Small wonder that the *Scribner's* editors found the story confusing.[6] Next to Poe and Faulkner, Cable is perhaps the most time-obsessed writer in American literature; but unlike Poe—and very like Faulkner—his renderings of chronology often are deliberately jumbled and misleading. It becomes clear in the course of the story that Cable's depiction of 'Sieur George began, as it were, in medias res. The reader is forced either to struggle to reconstruct an exact chronology of the story's events, or to be immersed in a fictional world so lax, so lethargic, that precise time really is of no consequence. The latter is most likely what Cable sought to achieve. The vagueness and confusion of time are a reflection of the vagueness of the Creole life and, more importantly, of 'Sieur George's disordered, depraved, shadowy existence.

These qualities are especially evident in Cable's handling of identity. " 'Sieur George" is not the protagonist's real name; it was given to him "at hazard" by some "merry serenaders" (250). In short, the so-called title is the joke of a group of singing pranksters, who despite—or because of—the "Monsieur" (later shortened by "the commoner people" to " 'Sieur" [250]) are treating him with profound disrespect. This use of the title "Monsieur" ironically to suggest a nonexistent nobility calls to mind Molière's comedy *L'Ecole des Femmes,* first performed in 1662 by his "Troupe de Monsieur." Cable's story seems to owe much to Molière's controversial play, whose protagonist's insistence that he be called "Monsieur de la Souche" rather than Seigneur Arnolphe is vital for the furtherance of plot and for the delineation of character. Cable's use of "Monsieur" achieves essentially the same ends, but the situation is compounded in the story by the use of "George." Without a terminal *s* ("Georges"), it is clearly what the Creoles would regard as an "Anglo" name, and Cable does broadly hint that the mysterious tenant is one of the scorned *Américains*. The ultimate American George is, of course, President Washington, who by virtue of Parson Weems's romanticized biography (ca. 1800) was already firmly established in the popular imagination as a quasi-mythical monument to honesty, dignity, and forthrightness.[7] Thus the very name "George"—like the title "Monsieur"—is an ironic joke.

Early on 'Sieur George (like the building he inhabits) began to exhibit "the symptoms of . . . decay": "Hints of a duel, of a reason warped, of disinheritance, and many other unauthorized rumors, fluttered up and floated off, while he became recluse, and, some say, began incidentally to betray the unmanly habit" of intemperance (249–50). In part, Cable is generating an enticing, romantic atmosphere in his story by speaking of duels, insanity, and disinheritance; but he undercuts that atmosphere by stating that these are "rumors"; and yet at the same time he counters the undercutting by emphasizing that the rumors are "unauthorized"—in short, they may be true. Similarly complex is the term "incidentally." Usually it means "by the way," but Cable has carefully avoided setting it off from the rest of the text by commas in the customary fashion; the omission of punctuation, coupled with the fact that it is used in conjunction with "the unmanly habit," implies that 'Sieur George's alcholism is an "incidental" part of a much larger, more serious pattern of personal degeneration. Typical of Cable's oblique style, he hints that there is more going on than he is willing to divulge; and likewise typical, the moment the reader's curiosity is piqued about George's shadowy private life, Cable offers a literary curve ball: " . . . one day 'Sieur George steps out of the old house in full regimentals!" (250).

Except for some early drinking with the "convivial fellows in regulation-blue" from the long-gone Fort St. Charles (250), there really is nothing in the story to prepare the reader for 'Sieur George's being an officer—or even a volunteer—in the army. It runs counter to the impression of deception and depravity that the author has been so diligently creating throughout the tale, and Cable capitalizes on the shock of the revelation by carefully rendering the reaction of the Creole tenants:

> The Creole neighbors rush bareheaded into the middle of the street, as though there were an earthquake or a chimney on fire. What to do or say or think they do not know; they are at their wits' ends, therefore well-nigh happy. However, there is a German blacksmith's shop near by, and they watch to see what *Jacob* will do. Jacob steps into the street with every eye upon him; he approaches Monsieur—he addresses to him a few remarks—they shake hands—they engage in some conversation—Monsieur places his hand on his sword!—now Monsieur passes.
> The populace crowd around the blacksmith, children clap their hands

softly and jump up and down on tip-toes of expectation—'Sieur George is
going to the war in Mexico! (251)

The quoted passage is far more vital than it might initially appear. First, it is
highly theatrical. Cable uses only the present tense of the verbs, thereby
imparting a dramatic immediacy to the passage. Likewise, the "tele-
graphed" passages separated (in an almost Dickinsonian fashion) by dashes
are evocative of a dumb show; this characteristically Cablesque device
conveys the infectious excitement, not only of the Creoles, but even of the
intrusive narrator. Even more importantly, it is quite apparent from this
scene that the nattily uniformed American soldier is not really a part of the
"bareheaded" Creole world. Whereas he (at least momentarily) exudes order
and sophistication, the Creoles come across as semicivilized, childlike, and
highly emotional.[8] In light of this, the reference to 'Sieur George's "Creole
neighbors" is essentially ironic. We had been told only a few paragraphs
earlier that although everyone lived in a single building, the Creoles "cut
him" many years before for being aloof (250). In short, their excitement
over him is more a matter of a temporary situation than a reappraisal and
acceptance of him; he is not, and can never be, one of them. That he is
distinct from the Creole world is further emphasized by the fact that it
required "Jacob" (both a Christian name and a generic term for a German)
to ascertain that 'Sieur George was going to fight in the Mexican wars. For
the native residents of New Orleans, any non-Creoles—Germans, *Américains,* whatever—were to be lumped together as the scorned "Anglos" who
were imposing themselves upon Louisiana. The blurring of identities (German or American, soldier or civilian) and the failure of communication that
the scene in the courtyard presents are clearly in keeping with Cable's study
of a man degenerating in a rather unsophisticated alien environment.

But once again typical of Cable, just as the reader might be tempted to
reappraise 'Sieur George to accommodate the new information about his
military career, the title character is essentially dropped from the story: "And
so years, and the Mexican war, went by" (253). As a sort of marker for the
absent protagonist, Cable introduces someone who is, in effect, 'Sieur
George's doppelgänger—"a youngish lady in black" who slips into his
apartment during the commotion in the courtyard, establishes residence
there for the duration of his absence, and zealously guards the little hair-
trunk that 'Sieur George had brought with him when he first moved into
Kookoo's building some fifteen years before (251–52). As with 'Sieur
George, the lady "chose mystery rather than society" (252), and the curious
landlord continues to be thwarted in his attempts to ascertain the contents of
trunk.

That trunk has been the focus of much critical controversy. Arlin Turner
perceives it as part of Cable's "straining for suspense," his reliance upon

"artificial concealment and contrivance of plot";[9] Claude M. Simpson argues that it is a unifying device comparable in importance to 'Sieur George himself.[10] To a certain extent both men are correct: our desire to see Kookoo's curiosity satisfied does compel us not to abandon the challenging experience of reading this grim tale, and the inclusion of recurring elements does much to counter the studied vagueness and complexity of Cable's distinctive style. But the hair-trunk achieves more than this. It is comparable to a controlling image in a fine poem, and its function as a technical device and its meaning as a symbol keep changing in the course of the story. On the most basic level, it functions as a treasure chest. Kookoo "should not soon forget that trunk. One day, fifteen years or more before, he had taken hold of that trunk to assist Monsieur to arrange his apartment, and Monsieur had drawn his fist back and cried to him to 'drop it!' " (252). The sudden inclusion of American slang in a passage redolent of the cadences of French is something of a shock, and it helps to render understandable the startled Kookoo's determination to fathom the trunk's mystery. His assumption that it is a treasure chest is, of course, reflective of Cable's desire to generate an aura of mystery; but this use of the trunk seems considerably less contrived when one realizes that the "youngish lady in black" guards the trunk zealously for many years—and that long after her death, 'Sieur George tells her daughter that " 'I frittered your poor, dead mother's fortune away' " (262). Cable leads us to believe—but never states overtly—that the trunk was indeed the repository of the woman's fortune—a veritable treasure chest. But more important than the money is the act of "frittering" it away. When Kookoo finally opens the trunk at the end of the story, it is found to be "full, full, crowded down and running over full, of the tickets of the Havana Lottery!" (266). Thanks to 'Sieur George, a trunk full of money became a trunk full of worthless paper—a situation reminiscent of Hawthorne's "Peter Goldthwaite's Treasure"[11] and, more recently, of Ike McCaslin's tin coffee pot full of IOU's in Faulkner's "The Bear" (part 4). It seems clear that the hair-trunk is a graphic emblem of 'Sieur George's moral degeneration. We are never told the nature of his relationship with the young woman, but it is apparent that her fortune (which is both inside, and symbolized by, the trunk) had been entrusted to his care—and that he violated that trust by steadily exchanging the money for lottery tickets. In a similar fashion, 'Sieur George degenerated from a young man "in full regimentals" who originally moved to the neighborhood because it was "very fashionable" (249), to a homeless, helpless old fool "trudging across the marshy commons, . . . following the sunset out upon the prairies to find a night's rest in the high grass" (267). Closely aligned with this, the trunk symbolizes 'Sieur George's progressively disordered psyche. He is a monomaniac, utterly unable to comprehend how he never won the Havana lottery after literally spending a fortune on tickets—" 'I don't see how I missed it!' " (263); and his obsessive guardianship of the trunk—appropriate when it was full of money, but progressively more inappropriate as it became filled with losing tickets—reflects this worsening neurosis. Even the changing exterior of the chest mirrors 'Sieur George's degeneration: "the little [hair-] trunk got very old and bald," as did its "dingy and threadbare" owner (254, 258). In effect, as the exterior and contents of the trunk worsened, so did the physical appearance and mind of its owner.

The degeneration of the trunk parallels the degeneration of 'Sieur George's relationships with the young lady and her daughter. We are never told the nature of 'Sieur George's relationship with the woman in black who occupied his apartment during the Mexican war. However, 'Sieur George reveals at the end of the story that he had a covenant with a man for whose death he was responsible, a covenant that he would "care for his offspring" (262). One may surmise, then, that the mystery lady was the dead man's daughter (hence her black attire), but this is never stated overtly. There is no question, on the other hand, that 'Sieur George loved her. It is with clear resentment that he accompanies "the tall gentleman" (257) during the latter's visits to court her; and 'Sieur George "changed from bad to worse" after their wedding (258), becoming garrulous, shiftless, and a drunkard. That he adopts their daughter after their untimely deaths is of vital importance. It is a reflection of his love for the child's mother, and it suggests that he is trying to honor the covenant; but such motivations, however commendable, do not lead to a commendable end: the old man proposes marriage to the girl he has raised as his daughter for sixteen years. She, understandably upset that her "Papa George" would entertain such a notion, "uttered a low, distressful cry, and, gliding swiftly into her room, for the first time in her young life turned the key between them" (264). Louis D. Rubin, Jr. is quite correct that this is a "startling dénouement," powerful in its "suggestion of near depravity" and its "furtive understatement."[12] No aspect of 'Sieur George's existence—his drinking, his gambling, his responsibility for a man's death, his squandering of a trusting woman's fortune—seems as reprehensible as his suggestion that this innocent young girl marry him. The scandalousness is comparable to that which surrounded the work and personal life of Molière (1622–73), whose 1662 comedy L'Ecole des Femmes (The School for Wives) may well have been an important literary source for " 'Sieur George.' "[13] In both Molière's play and Cable's story, the protagonist is a man with an assumed title, "Monsieur." Both Seigneur Arnolphe ("Monsieur de la Souche") and 'Sieur George had become guardians to female infants whom they raised to young adulthood. At the time they appear in their respective works, Agnès is seventeen years old, and the unnamed ward in " 'Sieur George" is sixteen. Each girl has been kept out of the mainstream of life: " . . . it's enough for her to know / How to spin, love me, say her prayers, and sew" says Arnolphe of Agnès;[14] and 'Sieur George could make the same appraisal of his convent-educated ward, whose only apparent talent is for embroidery (261). Further, despite the great disparity in ages, each guardian wishes to marry his ward—a situation that in both works seems virtually incestuous. This element takes on an added dimension when one considers the personal situation of Molière, whose play allegedly embodies what Brander Matthews delicately terms his "preoccupations at the moment of its composition."[15] To be precise, only eleven months before *L'Ecole des Femmes* was first produced, the forty-year-old Molière had married twenty-year-old Armande Béjart. She is believed to have been the sister of Madeleine Béjart, Molière's longtime colleague and business partner. Some argued, however, that Armande was actually the daughter of Madeleine—and since Madeleine had been the mistress of Molière for many years, there was the distinct possibility that the father of Armande was Molière himself. It is difficult to believe that the famed playwright would marry his own child, but the rumors of incest continued well into the twentieth century. Even so rational and sympathetic a biographer as John Palmer seems puzzled as he attempts to unravel the complicated emotional bases of the ill-fated marriage:

> The marriage of Molière may be summarized in brief simplicity. Molière loved Armande as a child. She was in a sense his ward, the favourite sister of Madeleine, whom she had come to regard as a mother. Her feeling for Molière, as she grew to maturity, may be easily imagined—gratitude towards the man to whom she owed her education, pride in the man who was becoming so famous, pleasure in the man who undoubtedly charmed and spoiled her with gifts. On the side of Molière was an indulgent affection for the child, which he never lost, to be gradually enlivened and intensified till it became the one serious passion of his life.
> Madeleine in this story is the friend of Molière, and, in effect, the mother of Armande. She had lost her daughter Françoise, and her youngest sister had for years been the sole outlet for her strong maternal instinct. For her the marriage of Armande and Molière was a union of the two beings for whom she had cared most in her life. They were the children of her inclination.[16]

The confusion of these three people's identities—father, mother, child, sister, mistress, wife, husband, guardian, ward—is reflected (on a small scale) in the Arnolphe/Agnès relationship in *L'Ecole des Femmes*; and it is precisely the sort of situation that would appeal to Cable, for whom the apparent arbitrariness of racial and national identity proved to be a lifelong preoccupation.

Whether or not Cable had in mind Molière's personal life and/or *L'Ecole des Femmes* as he wrote " 'Sieur George,"[17] the fact remains that the story ends on a coarse sexual note, and Rubin is probably correct that the *Scribner's* staff members were so enthralled by the exotic aura and novelty of the story's setting that "the underlying harshness of the material failed to register."[18] The harshness is not mitigated by the possibility that 'Sieur George (unlike Arnolphe) may not have raised his ward with the conscious intention of marrying her. He tearfully claims that he " 'always meant everything for the best' " (262); but he also admits that he " 'took' " her as an infant " 'for better or worse' " [sound familiar?] and that he had been planning to propose marriage for " 'a long time—for months' " (263). These admissions, coupled with his well-documented propensity for self-indulgence, hardly suggest the noblest intentions.

As the story closes, the young ward has concealed herself in a nearby convent, and 'Sieur George tries desperately to locate her—not to make amends, but to borrow ten dollars for one more try at the Havana lottery: "and there's an end" (267). Cable's portrait of a degenerate is uncompromising; and part of what makes it so powerful, so incisive, is the atmosphere that permeates the story. As has been suggested, " 'Sieur George" is structured around a series of recurring motifs: closure, concealment, lethargy, unclear identity, dubious sexuality. These motifs generate the aura of the exotic and the mysterious that is a donnée of the Creole world, especially as it is depicted in Cable's fiction. But it cannot be overlooked that 'Sieur George himself, for all his fifty years' residence in Kookoo's building, is not of that world; he is an *Américain*. There is thus a clear double standard in " 'Sieur George." For the Creoles, closure and concealment are matters of security and privacy. The impression one receives from this particular Cable story is that the worst these happy people have to hide is (quite literally) some damp laundry. In contrast, for 'Sieur George, closure is a matter of cutting himself off from his fellow man, and his efforts at concealment involve a lifetime of sins and mistakes—not wet clothes. Likewise, the lethargy of the Creoles is presented as charming, and it does not inhibit their ability to engage in meaningful work. Cable is careful to emphasize that Kookoo does manage to function as a landlord, and that the Creole tenants do have careers as "keepers in wine-warehouses, rent-collectors . . . , custom-house supernumeraries, and court-clerks' deputies" (248). Compared with the Creoles, 'Sieur George is shiftless and chronically unemployed. A similar double standard exists in regard to the unclear identities and dubious sexuality to be found in Creole society. One may assume that "Kookoo" is not the real name of the landlord, and we are told that he is "of doubtful purity of blood" (248), but these elements are simply taken for granted by the other Creoles. The uncertainty about Kookoo is part of what makes him a colorful individual, and the open acceptance of him indicates the relaxed atmosphere in which he lives. But what passes for normalcy among the Creoles is questionable when displayed by an American. 'Sieur George's pseudonym betokens serious flaws in his character, and his feelings for his young ward are hardly natural. Clearly Cable is suggesting that the very elements that constitute the most appealing aspects of the Creole world will bring out the worst, the most reprehensible, qualities in an American. In the seemingly lax society of early-nineteenth-century New Orleans, the Creoles were able to thrive precisely because they were in their natural environment; but introduce an outsider into that (comparatively speaking) semicivilized state, and he degenerates to the point where he begs money for lottery tickets and lusts after his adopted daughter. This degeneration of a civilized man in an alien, less sophisticated environment is precisely what Joseph Conrad would examine thirty years later in "Heart of Darkness," and it is what Herman Melville investigated some twenty-five years earlier in *Typee* and *Omoo*. What D. H. Lawrence writes of Melville's observations of white men in the South Pacific would apply equally well to Cable's observations of 'Sieur George in the world of the Creoles: "If you prostitute your psyche by returning to the savages, you gradually go to pieces. Before you can go back, you *have* to decompose. And a white man decomposing is a ghastly sight."[19] Cable, I suspect, would take issue only with the word "savages."

Cable's portrait of the degeneration of 'Sieur George is only heightened by the author's implied commentary at the end of the story. The orphaned girl contemplates New Orleans from the window of Mother Nativity asylum, where she is hiding from her adoptive guardian:

> Far away southward and westward the great river glistened in the sunset. Along its sweeping bends the chimneys of a smoking commerce, the magazines of surplus wealth, the gardens of the opulent, the steeples of a hundred sanctuaries and thousands on thousands of mansions and hovels covered the fertile birthright arpents which 'Sieur George, in his fifty years' stay, had seen tricked away from dull colonial Esaus by their blue-eyed brethren of the North. . . . [A]nd but a little way off, trudging across the marshy commons, her eye caught sight of 'Sieur George following the sunset out upon the prairies to find a night's rest in the high grass. (266–67)

The image of 'Sieur George in the high grass calls to mind another displaced individual, the biblical Esau, "a man of the field" (Gen. 25:27), and the personification of the nation of Edom. Esau was so named because "all his body [was] like a hairy mantle" (Gen. 25:25)—an element that perhaps makes clear why Cable chose to have 'Sieur George associated so insistently with a hair trunk. The biblical Esau sold his birthright to his younger twin in exchange for some food, and from then on was scorned by his father Isaac (who said "By your sword you shall live" [Gen. 27:40]), his people, and his Lord, who "stripped Esau bare [and] uncovered his hiding places": "he is no more" (Jer. 49:10). The degeneration of the biblical Esau helps clarify how we are to respond to the comment that the lands and wealth of New Orleans had been "tricked away from dull colonial Esaus by their blue-eyed brethren from the North." Fifty years earlier, 'Sieur George, an *Américain,* would have been counted among those "brethren from the North"; as such, he should have acquired the wealth, power, social prominence, and/or career success made possible by the wealth of the Delta. In effect, success in Louisiana would have been his "inheritance," as a Northerner. But 'Sieur George had been "tricked" out of that inheritance—and the trickster was himself. By immersing himself in the Creole world (even playing the Havana Lottery, that game promising unearned wealth—a concept so alien to the work-oriented Northern Protestant mind), 'Sieur George engineered his own degeneration, just as surely as dull-witted Esau willingly sold his birthright for some pottage. Had 'Sieur George continued to treasure his Northern Protestant "birthright"—including his work ethic—he would most likely have flourished, be it in the military, commerce, or any of the other avenues to success open to Northerners in newly acquired Louisiana. Indeed, 'Sieur George might have been as thriving as the blacksmith who served as his interpreter. One of the thousands of German immigrants (including the Cable family; the surname was originally Kobell, then Kable)[20] who arrived in New Orleans early in the nineteenth century with the intention of succeeding through hard work, the blacksmith was able to live in New Orleans *without* succumbing to the attractions of the comparatively unenterprising Creole society. Between the German's strong work ethic and the American's willingness to immerse himself in the Creole world, the latter lost out; and the symbolic blacksmith—appropriately named *Jacob* (251)—was able to acquire the "inheritance" that ostensibly should have gone to the American-born Esau, 'Sieur George. In part, then, Cable's story is a kind of veiled tribute to the German community, as well as to thousands of others from the North and Europe, who through diligence and foresight had played such an important role in the phenomenal growth of New Orleans into a commercial center and one of the largest seaports in America. But it also is a moral statement about the importance of hard work, the honoring of a covenant, the need to control one's self-indulgent impulses— in short, the importance of maintaining one's personal integrity despite the conditions under which one lives. As such, the story is perhaps also a parable, a symbolic imaginative projection of what might have happened to another George—Cable himself. It would have been so easy for him to write stories extolling the superficial charms of the Creole world, to ignore the harsh realities underlying the exotic exterior of that society, to pander to the popular tastes of his Northern readership and Creole neighbors—and to thrive in the process. But he chose the more challenging route, resisting the attractions of Creole life, risking the alienation of his neighbors in his plea for civil rights, and enduring financial hardships rather than compromising his vision.[21] George Washington Cable was no Esau. His birthright, his talent, and his integrity are evident on every page of *Old Creole Days.*

A Triangle of Transition:
"Madame Délicieuse"

E ARLY in 1878, as he revised and organized the stories that were to be published as *Old Creole Days* the following year, Cable entertained the notion of arranging the tales according to the dates when they took place, with "Jean-ah Poquelin" (set in 1805) coming first, and "'Sieur George" (1850) last. "These dates would be exactly correct, but maybe policy would dictate a more marketable arrangement of the stories. Putting Madame Délicieuse, for instance, as the best foot, foremost."[1] The marketability of "Madame Délicieuse" in the 1870s was undeniable. Pulished in *Scribner's Monthly Magazine* in August 1875, it proved to be a special favorite of editor Richard Watson Gilder; it was known "almost by heart" by Hjalmar Hjorth Boyesen, whose students at Cornell University would listen to him read it "with tears in their eyes"; English critic Edmund Gosse recommended it as a "perfectly original" picture of "the glittering, lazy, graceful life of the Creole population in its palmy days"; and even a reyiewer in the New Orleans *Times* felt that the story's Creole characters "could not fail to please" Cable's readily offended Creole readership.[2] Beloved by all and offensive to none, "Madame Délicieuse" would indeed have been an ideal opening for a collection of short stories, that maverick literary form that traditionally fares ill in the marketplace. It is difficult to believe, though, that so dedicated and serious an artist as Cable would mistake marketability for intrinsic literary worth, and so one may reasonably question his appraisal of "Madame Délicieuse" as his "best foot." Part of his high opinion of the story may be attributed to the fact that it embodies, in encapsulated form, all of the major themes, character types, and tensions that render *Old Creole Days* such a moving document of life in New Orleans during the fifty years following the Louisiana Purchase (1803). By placing "Madame Délicieuse" foremost in his story collection, Cable would thus be signifying its keynote status as a study of the social, political, cultural, and intellectual changes attendant upon New Orleans's painful transition from a discrete, static community with a prominent Creole element, to its submergence within the burgeoning, technically oriented entity known as America—changes that are insistent in every story in *Old Creole Days*. On a superficial level,

"Madame Délicieuse" is indeed "one of the most delicate, most whimsically gay" of Cable's stories;[3] but as Etienne de Planchard argues in a 1975 issue of *Caliban,* the story is more profitably perceived as an allegory of the clash between the old (Creole) order and the new (American) one. Remarkably, Cable chose to dramatize this clash—probably the single most important motif in Cable's literary canon—in terms of a romantic triangle involving a father, his son, and the woman they both love.[4]

The father is an ideal representative of the old Creole order. Even his very name—General Hercule Mossy de Villivicencio—reflects the combination of an imposing physical presence ("Hercules") and impeccable gentle breeding that are evident in all of the pure-blooded Creoles whom Cable presents in his fiction. Everything about General Villivicencio is larger than life; although Cable never describes him, we have a strong sense of his physicality, and especially of his unusual height. We first see him in a parade, "towering above his captains" (276); apparently never out of uniform, he seems particularly conscious of his sword and spurs (281, 283) and has the habit of tapping his fingers, which sound like "far-away drums" (286). His physicality and military orientation are particularly evident in his propensity for action. He does not hesitate to enter into a heated political campaign against the scorned *Américains* who continue to impose themselves upon the proud city, and immediately decides to duel when he feels he has been attacked in the newspapers. And at the same time that General Villivicencio is "a man's man," a dashing army officer and a political leader, he is a study in good breeding. Immensely wealthy, he is known throughout New Orleans for his "splendid alms" (274); both dashing and courtly, he is the cynosure of all female eyes as he rides in the Eighth of January parade;[5] and his relationship with Madame Clarisse Délicieuse, his "richly adorned and regal favorite" (273), is so wholesome that Clarisse's duenna does not hesitate to leave the two of them alone together (283). Physically imposing, action-oriented, generous, and chaste, General Villivicencio is almost a textbook example of Creole manliness; small wonder that Cable's Creole readership found no fault with him. But Villivicencio's impressive exterior and fine personal qualities do not mitigate several of his less impressive features—features that tend to humanize Villivicencio (thereby preventing him from seeming like a wooden character out of a fairy tale) while simultaneously acknowledging the less appealing aspects of the old Creole order that he represents. For example, his political activities are considerably less momentous than they might at first appear. His campaign against the Americans was doomed at the outset. The announcement in the papers that he would run for office was "greeted with profound gratification by a few old gentlemen in blue cottonade," who foresaw "a happy renaissance; a purging out of Yankee ideas; a blessed home-coming of those good old Bourbon morals and manners which Yankee notions had expatriated." But at the same time the announcement was greeted "by roars of laughter from a rampant majority" who perceived the General's supporters as "swarthy and wrinkled remnants of an earlier generation" (278, 284). Much as his political campaign is ludicrous, so is his military career. Cable makes it quite clear that he has not seen action since 1815; for the previous fifteen years—which is, significantly, the period during which he has not spoken with his son— Villivicencio has been a soldier without a war. His military action consists of riding in parades, where "with the gracious pomp of the old-time gentleman, [he] lifts his cocked hat, and bows, and bows" (276). In terms of both politics and military matters, then, Villivicencio is something of an anachronistic joke; and his inability to recognize this is attributable directly to his blind vanity. His unrealistically high sense of his personal worth is reflected in his relationship with the community at large. The newspaper article entitled "The Crayfish-eaters' Ticket," which attacks the General and the "fossils" who support him in his campaign (289), apparently is ignored by most of New Orleans, but the enraged Villivicencio claims that it "'surprised and exasperated'" the entire city and he can think of "but one way to settle" the insult: a duel (295). Likewise, his blind vanity also affects his romantic relationship with Madame Clarisse Délicieuse. He cannot perceive that she plays upon his feelings, that her flattery and lies control him with alarming ease. In a few minutes of conversation, she puts a major rift into the bitter stalemate that has existed between himself and his son for a decade and a half, and his "ecstatic complacency"—his automatic assumption that "the most martial-looking man in Louisiana" would of course be the ideal husband for "Louisiana's queenliest woman" (282–83)—leads to an embarrassingly unsuccessful marriage proposal that renders him "humbled, crestfallen, rejected!" (284). But nowhere is his blind vanity more apparent than in his relationship with his estranged son, Dr. Mossy.

Appropriate for a story that pits the old Creole order against the new American one, Villivicencio and his son function as foils. Whereas the father is an action-oriented man (albeit without a viable field of action), the son is bookish, reclusive, and thought oriented—what Merrill Maguire Skaggs aptly terms "a misfit in Creole society."[6] Since Louisiana was acquired by the stroke of a pen rather than military exploits, it is only fitting that the son—who, being approximately thirty years of age (271), is virtually an exact contemporary of the American presence in Louisiana—is almost always depicted in the story as writing at his desk. Cable underscores the split between the sword and the pen by providing the two characters with disparate attributes; whereas his father is associated with swords and spurs, Dr. Mossy is associated with writing instruments, manuscripts, books, and jars of specimens to study. Further, whereas the father has an inflated opinion of his reputation in the ineffectual, shrinking Creole community, Dr. Mossy—very much a product of the technology minded American order—is disarmingly modest about his bona fide reputation in the world of science, both here and abroad. As Clarisse reveals to General Villivicencio, " 'I could have told you some things too wonderful to believe. I could have told you that his name was known and honored in the scientific schools of Paris, of London, of Germany! . . . I could have shown you letters . . . written as between brother and brother, from the foremost men of science and discovery!' " (298) Further, while Villivicencio—so enamored of "appearances" in the Creole fashion[7]—prides himself on a bravery that is assumed but neither revealed nor tested, his son proves himself constantly in disease-ridden New Orleans, where he is " 'braver than *any soldier,* in tending the small-pox, the cholera, the fevers, and all those horrible things' " (281, Cable's emphasis).

All in all, Cable would seem to be stacking the proverbial deck in favor of the intellectual, famous, and selfless young doctor and, concomitantly, the new American world of which he is a representative; but true to form, Cable eschews presenting any character or situation in black and white terms. As with real fathers and sons, General Villivicencio and Dr. Mossy share certain features, often of the undesirable sort. Both men are too proud to make the first move toward reconciliation. It takes Clarisse, "playing the game of 'fausses confidences,' "[8] to trick them into interaction, and even then neither man shows any facility with communication. Typical of their relationship is the confusion over the revenge against the author of "The Crayfish-eaters' Ticket." Villivicencio assumes that his son will duel on his behalf, but "The peace-loving little doctor did not mean 'to settle,' but 'to adjust.' He felt in an instant that he was misunderstood; yet, as quiet people are apt to do, though not wishing to deceive, he let the misinterpretation stand" (294). As this misunderstanding suggests, what really undercuts Cable's positive presentation of Dr. Mossy is not what he shares with his father, but rather those unappealing features that are unique to him—features wherein his own father easily surpasses him. Much of what Cable reveals about Dr. Mossy suggests diminution. Whereas the General is a "plumed giant" (271), Dr. Mossy is short and spare: "A small blue-eyed, broad-browed, scholarly-looking man" (277). Cable underscores his diminutiveness by overloading the text with phrases suggestive of passivity and slightness: "the little Doctor" (287), "the quiet little Doctor" (292), "the gentle son" (287). His very name, "Dr. Mossy"—apparently a concession to Americans' inability to pronouce elaborate Gallic names—is a reduced version of "Hercule Mossy de Villivicencio." For that matter, even the disparity in their homes suggests diminution. The large, antiquated General lives, appropriately enough, in a "castle" (289); his son, in good American fashion, lives in a "little one-story, yellow-washed tenement" (271).[9] But probably the most strident disparity between father and son, the one area in which diminution is most marked, is in Cable's handling of the two men's sexuality. Everything about the General, from his unusual size to his sword, suggests an insistent masculinity; everything about Dr. Mossy suggests effeminacy. The young physician has "a modest, amiable, smile, very sweet and rare on a man's mouth" (271); he blushes inordinately, a quality remarked a striking number of times in such a brief story (e.g., 288, 293, 303); and when his father came to visit him at his office, Dr. Mossy rose "on tiptoe, laid his hand upon his father's shoulder, and lifting his lips like a little wife, kissed him" (285). The effeminacy of Dr. Mossy that Cable depicts in so uncompromising a fashion does much to illuminate the quarrel in which the General and his son have been engaged for fifteen years, a quarrel that evidently is primarily of the father's making. Madame Délicieuse, who attempts to fathom the sources of the conflict by bringing it into the open, suggests to the General that perhaps the problem is Dr. Mossy's shortness, and the lack of manliness that his somatotype ostensibly betokens: " 'It is just—because—he is—a little man!' " (282), not " 'big like a horse or quarrelsome like a dog' " (283). She also suggests that the quarrel had its origins in Dr. Mossy's childhood, when his father would spank him for refusing to play with his toy gun and drum (275–76). This refusal reflects (on a symbolic level) the new generation's recognition of the ascendancy of the American order that acquires territory by documents and money rather than military force. Closely aligned with this, on a more personal level it reflects Dr. Mossy's rejection of his father and all that his father represents—the aristocracy, a showy masculinity, and old money (Dr. Mossy has been disinherited). The long-lived, insistent tension between the father and son may suggest that the General does not perceive his son as being adequately "manly," and in fact he is not—that is, if one judges him by the almost impossibly high standards of a career army officer whose own young manhood was spent on the battlefield.[10] Aggression and violence simply are alien to Dr. Mossy's temperament and lifestyle, but a marriage—especially to someone of whom the General clearly approves—would at least confirm Dr. Mossy's status as the head of a household, the lord of a domestic manor. Hence the General's immediate blessing on his son's engagement to Clarisse, whom only a short time before the General had regarded as ideally suited to be his own wife. Whatever the case, the ending of the story—the resolution of the love triangle—is less satisfying than one might expect. Most of the problem is the character of Clarisse, whose ability to bridge the generation gap strains credulity, and whose character is oddly elusive.

In many respects, Clarisse is ideally suited to serve as the link between the old Creole and the new American order. Early in the story, Cable posits her as something of an archetypal Creole belle: "She never looked so like her sweet name, as when she seated her prettiest lady adorers close around her, and got them all a-laughing"; on parade days, she and her giggling entourage would assemble themselves upon balconies "to wave handkerchiefs and cast flowers" to the men in the procession, and to be admired by passers-by who "smiled at the ladies' eager twitter" as they "flirt[ed] in humming-bird fashion from one subject to another" (275). Further, as a Creole lady she makes ample use of the Catholic confessional, she is noted for her "kind offices and beneficent schemes," and at sixteen she was involved in an arranged marriage (273–74). The charming—albeit rather vacuous—girlishness that Clarisse exudes makes her an ideal symbol of Creole womanhood; she is very much a part of the world of which General Villivicencio is a sterling example, and as such his love for her is entirely understandable. But in order to have her function as the link between the General's world and his son's, Cable rather incredibly imparts to her several features that would have been stridently atypical of a Creole woman. For example, although she is "not such a sinner against time and place as to be an 'educated woman'" (274), she ostensibly has a sufficiently extensive knowledge of quite technical scientific matters to be able to appreciate Dr. Mossy's achievements as a researcher. Further, thanks to the "extravagant" act of visiting the city's American sector, she, like Dr. Mossy, has learned English (274)—what the General terms "'a vile tongue'" (292)—so as to be better able to communicate with the world outside of the limited Creole community. Likewise atypical of a Creole belle, she is intensely involved in politics and "similar freaks" (274); in fact, it is at her instigation that the General embarks on his campaign against the Americans. But the General's ill-fated campaign is symptomatic of a much larger pattern of Clarisse's non-Creole tendencies: she lies and manipulates others to an extent far beyond the limits acceptable in that elusive entity known as "charm." Clarisse plays upon the General's vanity to compel him to enter into the doomed anti-American campaign, and it is she who writes "The Crayfish-eaters' Ticket," viciously attacking him and his "fossil" supporters. Granted, her ultimate goal is commendable—the reconciliation of the father and son—but she waited fifteen years to pursue it, and her means were dubious at best, cruel at worst. Similarly, she invents conversations that she "reports" to the General in order to probe his attitude toward his son, and she even attributes to Dr. Mossy "certain kindly speeches of her own invention" (285) so as to encourage the General to visit him. There is something rather coarse in her determination to produce "material for her next confession" (282), especially when we find late in the story that her behavior was in part an affectation: her "lovely eyes" are "without any of that round simplicity which we have before discovered in them" (291). The qualities in Clarisse that render her quite atypical for a Creole woman often are exaggerated to the point where she seems masculine. As part of her flattery of the General, she asserts that she wishes "she was a man, that she might vote for him" (278); she is associated with militarism, as when "the General's compliment had foiled her thrust" (279) and she makes "a pretty fist" (280). But her masculinity is especially evident in her relationship with her fiancé, Dr. Mossy. As childhood playmates, Clarisse easily held sway over him:

> " . . . if I wanted some fun, I had only to pull his hair and run into the house; he would cry, and monsieur papa would come out with his hand spread open and"—
> Madame gave her hand a malicious little sweep, and joined heartily in the laugh which followed. (276)

The sexual role reversal—the pattern of a hoydenish Clarisse and a milquetoast Mossy—has continued into adulthood. As the story ends with the announcement of their engagement and the fragrance of orange blossoms, "Madame Délicieuse, for almost the first time in her life, and Dr. Mossy for the thousandth—blushed" (303). One may justifiably wonder what sort of married couple they will make. After all, there is something rather unappealing about Clarisse's ultimate motive in reconciling the father and son. As long as he was disinherited, Dr. Mossy would not marry her, and so the reconciliation effectively serves her own desire to wed again. Further, one may question what sort of husband will be the bookish, reclusive, absent-minded Dr. Mossy, who can derive intense excitement from reading "a thrilling chapter on the cuticle" (285). Perhaps Cable himself hinted at the sort of brave new world of Americanized New Orleans that this couple would help to usher in by making repeated references to the "jars, and jars, and jars" (271) of specimens in Dr. Mossy's office. Full of "serpents and hideous fishes and precious specimens of many sorts" (271), they are far from appealing; and their unattractiveness is only heightened by the disordered environment in which they are situated: "ten thousand odd scraps of writing-paper strewn with crumbs of lonely lunches, and interspersed with long-lost spatulas and rust-eaten lancets" (271–72). That Cable later refers to these specimens as "little Adams and Eves in zoölogical gardens" (286) may suggest that he perceives Mossy and Clarisse as symbolic of the first couple, who are destined to live in a world of *both* "serpents and innocents" (296). It is characteristic of Cable that, much as he saw the Creole General Villivicencio as simultaneously admirable and ludicrous, he perceived the Americanized Creole couple, Mossy and Clarisse, as both commendable and unattractive. For Cable, neither the old Creole order nor the new American one was necessarily flawless or superior to the other. Far from being a slight love story, "Madame Délicieuse" is a rich political and social document that is vital for an understanding of the complex world of antebellum Louisiana that Cable presents in all eight stories of *Old Creole Days*. In fact, Cable signifies the special importance of "Madame Délicieuse" by placing it in the second most prominent position in the collection—the very end.[11]

Notes

Introduction

1. Griffith T. Pugh, "George Washington Cable," *Mississippi Quarterly* 20, no. 2 (Spring 1967): 72.

2. Richard Chase, *The American Novel and Its Tradition* (Garden City, N.Y.: Doubleday, 1957), 167. Chase later indicates that "*Old Creole Days* and *Mme. Delphine,* among Cable's early writings, are well worth reading" despite their "rather gratuitous mystification about who is who and who is doing what" (169).

3. For example, "Belles Demoiselles Plantation" is included in Milton R. Stern and Seymour L. Gross, eds., *American Literature Survey: Nation and Region, 1860–1900* (New York: Viking, 1968), 110–25. " 'Sieur George" and "Posson Jone' " are included in Claude M. Simpson, ed., *The Local Colorists: American Short Stories, 1857–1900* (New York: Harper & Brothers, 1960), 256–88. "Jean-ah Poquelin" appears in Thomas Daniel Young, Floyd C. Watkins, and Richmond Croom Beatty, eds., *The Literature of the South* (Glenview, Ill.: Scott, Foresman, 1968), 556–70.

4. William Malone Baskervill, *Southern Writers: Biographical and Critical Studies* (Nashville, 1897; facs. rpt., New York: Gordian Press, 1970), 1:319; Edmund Gosse, Review of *Madame Delphine* [and other stories], *Saturday Review* (London) 52 (20 August 1881): 237–38, rpt. in Arlin Turner, ed., *Critical Essays on George W. Cable* (Boston: G. K. Hall, 1980), 31; "My Acquaintance with Cable," *Viestnik Europii* (May 1883), rpt. in *The Critic* 3 (1883): 317: [Robert Underwood Johnson], "Cable's 'Madame Delphine,' " *Scribner's Monthly Magazine* 22 (1881): 791.

5. Charles Dudley Warner, "On Mr. Cable's Readings," *Century* 26 (June 1883): 311–12.

6. Philip Butcher, *George W. Cable* (New York: Twayne, 1962), 165.

7. Charles DeKay, Review, "Cable's *Old Creole Days,"* *Scribner's Monthly Magazine* 18 (July 1879): 473.

8. Griffith T. Pugh, "George W. Cable's Theory and Use of Folk Speech," *Southern Folklore Quarterly* 24, no. 4 (December 1960): 287–93; Edward Larocque Tinker, "Cable and the Creoles," *American Literature* 5, no. 4 (January 1934): 313–26.

9. Arlin Turner, *George W. Cable: A Biography* (Baton Rouge: Louisiana State University Press, 1966); Louis D. Rubin, Jr., *George W. Cable: The Life and Times of a Southern Heretic* (New York: Pegasus, 1969); Butcher, see note 6. Other valuable works pertaining to Cable include Kjell Ekström, *George Washington Cable: A Study of His Early Life and Work,* The American Institute in the University of Upsala, Essays and Studies on American Language and Literature, vol. 10 (Upsala and Cambridge: Harvard University Press, 1950); Lucy Leffingwell Cable Biklé, *George W. Cable: His Life and Letters* (New York: Charles Scribner's Sons, 1928); and Turner, ed., *Critical Essays,* which is a collection of reviews and analyses. A good brief overview of Cable's life and work is offered by Edmund Wilson, "The Ordeal of George Washington Cable," *The New Yorker* 33 (9 November 1957): 180–96, 201–18,

221–28; this material was incorporated into Wilson's *Patriotic Gore: Studies in the Literature of the American Civil War* (New York: Farrar, Straus and Giroux, 1977).

10. Writes Cable, ". . . there seems to be no more serviceable definition of the Creoles of Louisiana than this: that they are the French-speaking, native portion of the ruling class" (*The Creoles of Louisiana* [New York: Charles Scribner's Sons, 1884], 42). Cable never uses the word "Creole" to refer to an individual of mixed blood, although he notes that "the term was adopted by—not conceded to—the natives of mixed blood, and is still so used among themselves" (41). Edmund Wilson notes that the "Creole" language "is an Afro-French patois spoken by the Negroes of Louisiana, French Guiana and the French West Indies," but remarks that a true Creole is "a white colonial of French or Spanish blood" (*Patriotic Gore,* 557n). The confusion surrounding the term "Creole" is explored by Alice Dunbar-Nelson, "People of Color in Louisiana: Part I," *Journal of Negro History* 1, no. 4 (1916): 366–67; Oliver Evans, "Melting Pot in the Bayous," *American Heritage* 15 (December 1963): 32; and Grace King, *New Orleans: The Place and the People* (New York: Macmillan Company, 1904). Even though Cable clearly felt that Creoles had no Negro blood, a widespread and tenacious belief arose that he had insinuated in his writings that they were less than pure Caucasians. The difficulties this misunderstanding generated are explored in Tinker, "Cable and the Creoles," and Ekström, *Early Life and Work,* esp. chaps. 11 and 14.

11. For discussions of the Code Noir, see Alice Dunbar-Nelson, "People of Color," 364ff.; Evans, "Melting Pot in the Bayous," 49–50; and Robert O. Stephens, "Cable's *Madame Delphine* and the Compromise of 1877," *Southern Literary Journal* 12, no. 1 (Fall 1979): 80. The postwar Black Codes are discussed in Kenneth A. Stampp, *The Era of Reconstruction, 1865–1877* (New York: Alfred A. Knopf, 1969).

12. For an analysis of the term "local color," see my essay entitled "Universal and Particular: The Local-Color Phenomenon Reconsidered," *American Literary Realism: 1870–1910* 12, no. 1 (Spring 1979): 111–26.

13. Ekström, *Early Life and Work,* 42.

14. Turner, *A Biography,* 41–42.

15. Ibid., p. 41.

16. Ibid., p. 88; Cable to Fred Lewis Pattee, 21 July 1914, in Biklé, *Life and Letters,* 47.

17. Daniel Hoffman, *Poe Poe Poe Poe Poe Poe Poe* (New York: Avon, 1978), 268, 218.

18. Ekström, *Early Life and Work,* 42; letter dated 21 July 1914, in Biklé, *Life and Letters,* 47.

19. Ekström, *Early Life and Work,* 42; Turner, *A Biography,* 88.

20. Cable himself acknowledged that his refusal to review the play for the *Picayune* "would not have been cause for dismissal if his general performance as a news reporter had been more competent: 'I had neither the faculty for getting more news, nor the relish for blurting out news for news' sake after it was got. . . . I wanted to be always writing, and they wanted me to be always reporting.' In any event, during the summer of 1871 it was suggested to Cable that his resignation would be accepted, whereupon he went back to bookkeeping, vowing never to have anything to do with a newspaper again" (Rubin, *Southern Heretic,* 37).

21. Turner, *A Biography,* 88.

22. Turner argues that Cable, like Howells and James, had learned the dramatic method from Hawthorne and Turgenev (*A Biography,* 91). Although Turner is specifically discussing *The Grandissimes,* his observation applies equally well to the stories of *Old Creole Days.*

23. Cable to Louise Bartlett Cable, 27 October 1883, quoted in Rubin, *Southern Heretic*, 129.

24. Turner, *A Biography*, 57.

25. For an excellent discussion of Cable's church-related activities and his changing attitudes toward organized religion, see Turner, *A Biography*, chap. 20, "Religion and Culture."

26. Cable to Louise Bartlett Cable, 11 February 1901, quoted in Turner, *A Biography*, 279.

27. In his 1887 speech entitled "Cobwebs in the Church," Cable "protested that undue veneration was demanded and given to everything associated with the church, so much at times as to obscure the truths of religion. He protested against the scholastic approach to matters of religious belief, and also against the commercialism of rented pews and the atmosphere of exclusiveness which in effect barred strangers as well as lower social classes. The churches had ceased to be public institutions, he said, and had become agencies for 'private hospitality' and 'clique benevolence.' After hearing him read this paper before the New York Congregational Club, a later speaker remarked, 'I do pity the cobwebs when Mr. Cable gets after them.' After teaching one of his last classes in Boston, he wrote in his diary: 'They were much pleased with the lesson. I was not. They have an average religion that is water-logged with last century bilge-water.' " (Turner, *A Biography*, 279)

28. William Rodney Allen points out that various critics "have noted parallels between O'Connor's work and Hawthorne's—an insistence on man's fallen nature, a use of allegory, a departure from realism into the mode of the romance" ("Mr. Head and Hawthorne: Allusion and Conversion in Flannery O'Connor's 'The Artificial Nigger,' " *Studies in Short Fiction* 21 [Winter 1984]: 17). Allen's article traces the persistent echoes of Hawthorne's "The Custom House" in "The Artificial Nigger." Frederick Asals notes that O'Connor particularly admired Hawthorne's " 'lean' fiction as against the 'cumbersome' British novel of manners" (*Flannery O'Connor: The Imagination of Extremity* [Athens: University of Georgia Press, 1982], 161).

29. Cable to William Dean Howells, 8 October 1881, in Biklé, *Life and Letters*, 72–73.

30. Rubin, *Southern Heretic*, 122.

31. Fred Lewis Pattee, *A History of American Literature Since 1870* (New York: Century, 1915), 249.

32. See Arlin Turner, "A Novelist Discovers a Novelist: The Correspondence of H. H. Boyesen and George W. Cable," *Western Humanities Review* 5 (Autumn 1951): 365. Boyesen, a Norwegian writer and critic teaching at Columbia University, was one of Cable's earliest admirers. It was he who facilitated the publication of *Old Creole Days* by personally guaranteeing Blair Scribner against publishing losses. For the circumstances surrounding the volume's publication, see ibid., 351ff.; Butcher, *George W. Cable*, 26–30; and Biklé, *Life and Letters*, 56–59.

Old Creole Days was published on 17 May 1879 and sold unusually well for a collection of short stories. Within a month, 250 copies had been sold in New Orleans alone, and after only three months the first printing of 1,000 copies was exhausted (Rubin, *Southern Heretic*, 73). In 1920—more than forty years after *Old Creole Days* was first published—the volume sold more than 500 copies (Butcher, *George W. Cable*, 165). Edmund Wilson notes that the collection ran through seven editions between 1883 and 1937 (*Patriotic Gore*, 556).

Chapter 1. "Dey's Quadroons"

1. Cable recounts the incident in his Preface to *Madame Delphine* (New York: Charles Scribner's Sons, 1896), v–viii.

2. Ibid., viii.

3. *Madame Delphine* definitely lacks the scope and complexity of *The Grandissimes,* which had been published a year earlier. However, there is some evidence that the novella was begun before Cable's masterpiece. Arlin Turner argues that Cable began to write *Madame Delphine* as early as 1875: "The long interval before he finished the story may be explained by his unwillingness to write for the pay he received and some reluctance to argue the cause of the quadroons as directly as he planned in the story" (*George W. Cable: A Biography* [Baton Rouge: Louisiana State University Press, 1966], 105n). I would suggest that *Madame Delphine* be perceived as a transitional work between the other stories of *Old Creole Days* and *The Grandissimes.*

4. Robert O. Stephens, "Cable's *Madame Delphine* and the Compromise of 1877," *Southern Literary Journal* 12, no. 1 (Fall 1979): 87–88.

5. Consider the use of the word "fondly" in the following passage from " 'Tite Poulette": "About this time Kristian Koppig lost his position in the German importing house where, he had fondly told his mother, he was indispensable" (226).

6. William Bedford Clark, "Cable and the Theme of Miscegenation in *Old Creole Days* and *The Grandissimes,*" *Mississippi Quarterly* 30, no. 4 (Fall 1977): 609.

7. Lafcadio Hearn discusses the prototype of Madame Delphine's house in "The Scenes of Cable's Romances," *Century* 27 (November 1883): 44.

8. A "quadroon" is one-fourth black; an "octoroon" is one-eighth black (i.e., the child of a quadroon and a Caucasian). For a discussion of the elaborate system of racial labels for those of mixed blood, see Grace King, *New Orleans: the Place and the People* (New York: Macmillan 1904), chap. 14.

9. Cable's advocacy of Negro rights was based upon his study of the Bible, United States history (especially the Constitution), and his personal observations; but his public pronouncements of his position caused fellow Southerners to doubt Cable's mental stability. For example, he called for public school integration in print as early as 1875; but his radical ideas and inflammatory writing style rendered at least one of his editorials literally unpublishable (Turner, *A Biography,* 77). His public statements on the racial issue did not mitigate the situation. In 1887, the *Christian Advocate,* the official publication of the Methodist Episcopal Church, South, expressed dismay over a speech Cable delivered at Vanderbilt University, in which he called for full civil rights (including free education) for blacks: "A remarkable address it was—remarkable in the choice of topic, remarkable in what he felt called upon to say, remarkable in his apparent obliviousness to existing facts." The *Advocate* noted further that the deductions Cable made from widely accepted "political axioms" (the importance of patriotism; majority rule) were incomprehensible to the rational mind: their "relevancy might be apparent to a genius or a poet" but it was "not visible to the common sense of the men and women who sat and listened" with "astonishment at [Cable's lack of] logic." (Philip Butcher, *George W. Cable: The Northampton Years* [New York: Columbia University Press, 1959], 19–20) Small wonder that the most open-minded characters of *Madame Delphine* were seen as mentally unbalanced.

10. Michael L. Campbell, "The Negro in Cable's *The Grandissimes,*" *Mississippi Quarterly* 27, no. 2 (Spring 1974): 167.

11. Jay B. Hubbell discusses Cable's deterioration as an artist in *The South in American Literature: 1607–1900* (Durham, N.C.: Duke University Press, 1954), 819–20. See also Edward L. Tinker, "Cable and the Creoles," *American Literature* 5 (January 1934): 313–26. To quote Tinker, Cable's "pedagogic excesses murdered his creative ability. Renan declared that saints are usually dull people, and he might have added propagandists as well. Cable became a dull writer, his novels, prosy, platitudinous and choked with copybook morality" (325).

12. Cable to William Dean Howells, 8 October 1881, cited in Lucy Leffingwell Cable Biklé, *George W. Cable: His Life and Letters* (New York: Charles Scribner's Sons, 1928), 72–73.

13. Louis D. Rubin, Jr., *George W. Cable: The Life and Times of a Southern Heretic* (New York: Pegasus, 1969), 102.

14. The concept of the celestial account book may have been drawn from Cable's knowledge of Puritan religious thought. See Perry Miller, *Errand into the Wilderness* (Cambridge: Harvard University Press, 1975), chap. 3, "The Marrow of Puritan Divinity," esp. 81ff. Cable's mother was of old New England stock, and his values reflected his puritanical upbringing.

15. William Malone Baskervill, "George W. Cable," *Chautauquan* 25 (May 1897): 183; also in Baskervill's *Southern Writers: Biographical and Critical Studies* (Nashville, 1897; facs. rpt., New York: Gordian Press, 1970), 1:330.

16. Rubin, *Southern Heretic,* 101.

17. Jules Zanger, "The 'Tragic Octoroon' in Pre–Civil War Fiction," *American Quarterly* 18, no. 1 (Spring 1966): 63.

18. Oddly enough, Cable noted that Olive was the only character in *Madame Delphine* to be based upon a living individual. See his "After-Thoughts of a Story-Teller," *North American Review* 158, no. 446 (January 1894): 20.

19. As Thomas Hubert notes in his unfortunately brief essay entitled "The Gardens of *Old Creole Days*," jasmine is "a traditional symbol of the Virgin Mary." Olive's insistent association with jasmine suggests that she, like Pauline D'Hemecourt in "Café des Exilés," is "an embodiment of feminine beauty and purity tinged with holiness." ("The Gardens of *Old Creole Days*," *Revue de Louisiane/ Louisiana Review* 9 [1980]: 159) Cable often associates innocent young females with mockingbirds, including Olive, Pauline D'Hemecourt, and 'Tite Poulette. The mockingbird's traditional status as an embodiment of innocence and endearment is particularly apparent in Harper Lee's *To Kill a Mockingbird* (1960).

20. Edmund Gosse [Review of *Madame Delphine* [and other stories], *Saturday Review* (London) 52 (20 August 1881): 237–38, cited in Arlin Turner, ed., *Critical Essays on George W. Cable* (Boston: G. K. Hall, 1980), 30.

21. Stephens, "*Madame Delphine* and the Compromise," 90.

22. [Robert Underwood Johnson], "Cable's " 'Madame Delphine,' " *Scribner's Monthly Magazine* 22 (September 1881): 791.

23. Rubin, *Southern Heretic,* 102.

24. "Recent Novels," *The Nation* 33 (21 July 1881): 55.

25. Philip Butcher, *George W. Cable* (New York: Twayne, 1962), 58–59.

26. Review of *Madame Delphine, Literary World* 12 (30 July 1881): 259; rpt. in Turner, ed., *Critical Essays,* 26–27.

27. Cited in Turner, *A Biography,* 108.

28. See note 24 above.

29. Review of *Madame Delphine, The Critic* 1, no. 14 (16 July 1881); Baskervill, *Southern Writers,* 328; Turner, ed., *Critical Essays,* 28.

30. See Turner, *A Biography,* 324–25, 345, 354. Benjamin B. Hampton of Great Authors Pictures, Inc. was forced to shelve the film project because distributors were wary of the racial issue.

Chapter 2. *"Floating in the Clouds of Revery"*

1. Charles DeKay, Review, "Cable's *Old Creole Days*," *Scribner's Monthly Magazine* 18 (July 1879): 472.

2. Arlin Turner, *George W. Cable: A Biography* (Baton Rouge: Louisiana State University Press, 1966), 62.

3. DeKay, "Cable's *Old Creole Days*," 472–73.

4. Turner, *A Biography*, 62.

5. Cable to Scribner, Armstrong, & Co., 9 February 1878, cited in Lucy Leffingwell Cable Biklé, *George W. Cable: His Life and Letters* (New York: Charles Scribner's Sons, 1928), 58.

6. See Lafcadio Hearn, "The Scenes of Cable's Romances," *Century Magazine* 27 (November 1883): 45. Hearn's article includes a sketch of the model of D'Hemecourt's café on Rampart Street.

7. ". . . Cable himself seems to make certain class distinctions in his stories. One class for which he has little respect is composed of the Spanish Creoles." (Merrill Maguire Skaggs, *The Folk of Southern Fiction* [Athens: University of Georgia Press, 1972], 174)

8. Cable had a special fondness for Malory's *Morte d'Arthur;* reportedly he recommended the book to Samuel Clemens, who was inspired by it to write *A Connecticut Yankee in King Arthur's Court* (Turner, *A Biography*, 173).

9. Philip Butcher, *George W. Cable* (New York: Twayne, 1962), 40.

10. Turner, *A Biography*, 62.

11. Ibid., 63.

Chapter 3. The Fall of the House of De Charleu

1. "The Fall of the House of Usher" in *The Complete Tales and Poems of Edgar Allan Poe* (New York: Vintage, 1975), 232. All further references to Poe's writings are to this edition.

2. Philip Butcher suggests also that "readers who seek symbols and analogues . . . may take the fall of the house of De Charleu as a symbol for Creole New Orleans engulfed by a river of energetic Anglo-Saxons" (*George W. Cable* [New York: Twayne, 1962], 38). Although there may be some basis for this sociocultural reading, it seems more fruitful to approach the story as a religious allegory.

3. Donald A. Ringe, "The Moral World of Cable's 'Belles Demoiselles Plantation,'" *Mississippi Quarterly* 29 (Winter 1975–76): 85. Thomas Hubert notes that "Strictly speaking, the reference to the century plant may not be ironic or intended to be so, for it actually lives only ten or more years. Before it dies, it blooms, and new plants develop from suckers." ("The Gardens of *Old Creole Days*," *Revue de Louisiane / Louisiana Review* 9 [1980]: 155–56, n. 3.)

4. Hubert, "Gardens of *Old Creole Days*," notes that the violet is "traditionally emblematic of humility" (155). De Charleu's association with it is thus ironic.

5. Nathaniel Hawthorne, *The House of the Seven Gables* (Boston: Houghton Mifflin, 1964), 9.

6. Lafcadio Hearn, "The Scenes of Cable's Romances," *Century Magazine* 27 (November 1883): 47.

7. Howard W. Fulweiler, "Of Time and the River: 'Ancestral Nonsense' vs. Inherited Guilt in Cable's 'Belles Demoiselles Plantation,'" *Midcontinent American Studies Journal* 7 (Fall 1966): 54.

8. Ibid., 55.

9. Ibid., 58.

10. Ringe, "Moral World," 85.

11. Ibid., 90.

12. *The Book of Common Prayer* (Greenwich, Conn.: Seabury, 1953), 69.

13. Although it would be fruitless to attempt to establish a one-to-one correspondence between them, it seems possible that there are seven daughters because De Charleu has committed the Seven Deadly Sins:

1. Pride: As the "bitter-proud" (124) De Charleu daydreams about the proposed home in the city, he muses that "It should be the finest in the State. Men should never pass it, but they should say—'the palace of the De Charleus; a family of grand descent, a people of elegance and bounty, a line as old as France, a fine old man, and seven daughters as beautiful as happy; whoever dare attempt to marry there must leave his own name behind him!'" (126)
2. Wrath: De Charleu routinely becomes furious in his negotiations for the block owned by Injin Charlie. He "longed to blaspheme" in his frustration, and made "an ugly whisk at [Charlie] with his riding-whip" (133, 134).
3. Envy: De Charleu desperately desires the property owned by Charlie: "Lots, buildings, rents, all, might as well be his, he thought, to give, keep, or destroy" (125).
4. Lust: "He had had his vices," reportedly "all his life"; he had "danced and quarrelled at the St. Philippe-street theatre quadroon balls" (123–24). The sexual significance of quadroon balls is apparent to any reader of Cable's "'Tite Poulette."
5. Gluttony: Although Cable never depicts De Charleu eating, he does emphasize his legendary "bounty" and "voluptuous ease" (124, 136).
6. Avarice: Consider De Charleu's obsession to "engross the whole estate under one title" at the least possible price (125), in contrast to Injin Charlie's ability to "more than maintain" his household on the income from some dilapidated buildings (125).
7. Sloth: De Charleu is characterized by "luxurious idleness" (125).

14. Ringe, "Moral World," 85.
15. Ibid., 85, n. 5.
16. The reference to the glowworm and the emphasis on the theatricality of the story's climactic scene may call to mind two works by Poe: the poem "The Conqueror Worm" and the tale "The Masque of the Red Death," in which a play and a masque are unexpectedly disrupted by violent death. The staged quality of the drownings is also reminiscent of "Sketch Eighth: Norfolk Isle and the Chola Widow" in Herman Melville's "The Encantadas." In that sketch, the Chola widow Hunilla recounts how she helplessly watched as her husband and brother drowned

> Before Hunilla's eyes they sank. The real woe of this event passed before her sight as some sham tragedy on the stage. She was seated on a rude bower among the withered thickets, crowning a lofty cliff, a little back from the beach. The thickets were so disposed, that in looking upon the sea at large she peered out from among the branches as from the lattice of a high balcony. But upon the day we speak of here, the better to watch the adventure of those two hearts she loved, Hunilla had withdrawn the branches to one side and held them so. They formed an oval frame, through which the bluely boundless sea rolled like a painted one. And there, the invisible painter painted to her view the wave-tossed and disjointed raft, its once level logs slantingly upheaved, as raking masts, and the four struggling arms undistinguishable among them; and then all subsided into smooth-flowing creamy waters, slowly drifting the splintered wreck; while first and last, no sound of any sort was heard. Death in a silent picture; a dream of the eye; such vanishing shapes as the mirage shows.
>
> So instant was the scene, so trance-like its mild pictorial effect, so distant from her blasted bower and her common sense of things, that Hunilla gazed and gazed, nor raised a finger or a wail. But as good to sit thus dumb, in stupor staring on that dumb show, for all that otherwise might be done. ("The Encantadas; or, Enchanted Islands," in *Piazza Tales*, ed. Egbert S. Oliver [New York: Hendricks House, 1948], 183–84; "The Encantadas" appeared in *Putnam's Monthly Magazine* in Spring 1854.)

17. *Tales and Poems of Poe*, 238.
18. Edmund Gosse, Review of *Madame Delphine* [and other stories], *Saturday Review* (London) 52 (20 August 1881): 237–38, cited in Arlin Turner, ed., *Critical Essays on George W. Cable* (Boston: G. K. Hall, 1980), 31.

19. Louis D. Rubin, Jr., *George W. Cable: The Life and Times of a Southern Heretic* (New York: Pegasus, 1969), 52.

20. Fulweiler, "Time and the River," 58.

21. Kjell Ekström, *George Washington Cable: A Study of His Early Life and Work,* The American Institute in the University of Upsala, Essays and Studies on American Language and Literature, vol. 10 (Upsala and Cambridge: Harvard University Press, 1950), 42.

Chapter 4. The Story of the True Christian(s)

1. See Robert Underwood Johnson, *Remembered Yesterdays* (Boston: Little, Brown 1923), 123.

2. Cited in Arlin Turner, *George W. Cable: A Biography* (Baton Rouge: Louisiana State University Press, 1966), 63.

3. Edmund Gosse, Review of *Madame Delphine* [and other stories], *Saturday Review* (London) 52 (20 August 1881): 237–38, cited in Arlin Turner, ed., *Critical Essays on George W. Cable* (Boston: G. K. Hall, 1980), 31; Charles Dudley Warner, "On Mr. Cable's Readings," *Century* 26 (June 1883): 311; W. M. Baskervill, "George W. Cable," *Chautauquan* 25 (May 1897): 181; "Some Recent Novels," *Atlantic* 88 (December 1901): 847.

4. Claude M. Simpson, ed.; *The Local Colorists: American Short Stories, 1857–1900* (New York: Harper & Brothers, 1960), 257; Louis D. Rubin, Jr., *George W. Cable: The Life and Times of a Southern Heretic* (New York: Pegasus, 1969), 40; Turner, *A Biography,* 63.

5. Cable to Scribner, Armstrong, & Co, 9 February 1878, cited in Lucy Leffingwell Cable Biklé, *George W. Cable: His Life and Letters* (New York: Charles Scribner's Sons, 1928), 58.

6. F Scott Fitzgerald, "The Jelly-Bean," in *Six Tales of the Jazz Age, and Other Stories* (New York: Charles Scribner's Sons, 1960), 17. For an examination of this story as a study of the clash between the Old South and the new, see my "Love Story: Mock Courtship in F Scott Fitzgerald's 'The Jelly-Bean,'" *Arizona Quarterly* 39 (Fall 1983): 251–60.

7. Simpson, *Local Colorists,* 257.

8. *"Posson Jone'" and Père Raphaël, with a New Word Setting Forth How and Why the Two Tales are One,* illus. Stanley M. Arthurs (New York: Charles Scribner's Sons, 1909), 10. Patrick Samway, S.J., explores further "how and why the two tales are one" in "Cable's 'Posson Jone'' and 'Père Raphaël': 'Tis a Matt of Conscien'," *Revue de Louisiane/Louisiana Review* 11 (Summer 1982): 61–72.

9. Simpson, *Local Colorists,* 257.

10. Philip Butcher, *George W. Cable* (New York: Twayne, 1962), 117.

11. Jones is referring to the rule of the Messiah as it is depicted in Isaiah 11:6–7:

> The wolf shall dwell with the lamb,
> and the leopard shall lie down with the kid,
> and the calf and the lion and the fatling together,
> and the little child shall lead them.
> The cow and the bear shall feed;
> their young shall lie down together;
> and the lion shall eat straw like the ox.

12. The text as it originally appeared in *Appleton's Journal* (1 April 1876) reads as follows: "But the fascinations of Colossus's eloquence must not mislead us; this is the

story of Parson Jones" (423). The revised text reads, "But the fascinations of Colossus's eloquence must not mislead us; this is the story of a true Christian; to wit, Parson Jones" (157). Cable's revisions obviously were intended to emphasize the religious dimension of the story.

13. In retrospect, the previous reference to Colossus as "the black man" (162)—a term that traditionally (especially in Hawthorne) refers to the devil—is a typically Cablesque racial-religious pun, intentionally fraught with irony.

14. *"Posson Jone' " and Père Raphaël,* 12.

15. Warner, "On Mr. Cable's Readings," 311–12; Turner, *A Biography,* 138, 306. For discussions of the tours, see Guy A. Cardwell, *Twins of Genius* (East Lansing: Michigan State University Press, 1953) or Arlin Turner, *Mark Twain and George W. Cable* (East Lansing: Michigan State University Press, 1960).

16. Charles DeKay, Review, "Cable's *Old Creole Days,"* *Scribner's Monthly Magazine* 18 (July 1879): 473: "It seems a pity not to use the story . . . for the drama." See also Turner, *A Biography,* 324–25.

17. [Robert Underwood Johnson], "Cable's *Madame Delphine,"* *Scribner's Monthly Magazine* 22 (September 1881): 791.

Chapter 5. A Fable of Love and Death

1. William Dean Howells, *The Great Modern American Stories* (New York: Boni and Liveright, 1920), xi, cited in Arlin Turner, *George W. Cable: A Biography* (Baton Rouge: Louisiana State University Press, 1966), 61, n. 10.

2. Louis D. Rubin, Jr., *George W. Cable: The Life and Times of a Southern Heretic* (New York: Pegasus, 1969), 57; Edmund Wilson, *Patriotic Gore: Studies in the Literature of the American Civil War* (New York: Farrar, Straus and Giroux, 1977), 557n; and especially Edward Larocque Tinker, "Cable and the Creoles," *American Literature* 5, no. 4 (January 1934): 313–26.

3. Edward Stone, "Usher, Poquelin, and Miss Emily: The Progress of Southern Gothic," *Georgia Review* 14, no. 4 (Winter 1960): 433.

4. Turner, *A Biography,* 84.

5. John Cleman, "College Girl Wildness: Nature in the Work of George Washington Cable," *Markham Review* 5 (Winter 1976): 27.

6. Joseph J. Egan, " 'Jean-ah Poquelin': George Washington Cable as Social Critic and Mythic Artist," *Markham Review* 2, no. 3 (May 1970): [6]. Lafcadio Hearn discusses the prototype of Poquelin's house in "The Scenes of Cable's Romances," *Century Magazine* 27 (November 1883); 40.

7. Egan, " 'Jean-ah Poquelin,' " [7].

8. Joseph J. Egan, "Lions Rampant: Agricola Fusilier and Bras-Coupé as Antithetical Doubles in *The Grandissimes,"* *Southern Quarterly* 18, no. 4 (Summer 1980): 74.

9. Rubin, *Southern Heretic,* 56.

10. Michael L. Campbell, "The Negro in Cable's *The Grandissimes,"* *Mississippi Quarterly* 27, no. 2 (Spring 1974): 166.

11. See note 3 above; Bill Christophersen, " 'Jean-ah Poquelin': Cable's Place in Southern Gothic," *South Dakota Review* 20 (Summer 1982): 55–66.

12. Herbert G. May and Bruce M. Metzger, *The New Oxford Annotated Bible* (New York: Oxford University Press, 1973), 1179–80, note for Matthew 8:1–9:38.

13. Fred Lewis Pattee, *A History of American Literature since 1870* (New York: Century, 1915), 249.

Chapter 6. The Taint of Caste

1. See Cable's account in Lucy Leffingwell Cable Biklé, *George W. Cable: His Life and Letters* (New York: Charles Scribner's Sons, 1928), 45.

2. Arlin Turner suggests that " 'Tite Poulette" was "possibly a reworking of the sketch in the *Picayune* entitled 'A Life-Ebbing Monography' " (*George W. Cable: A Biography* [Baton Rouge: Louisiana State University Press, 1966], 59). Although " 'Tite Poulette" was one of the first stories Cable wrote, it was the third to be published in *Scribner's* (8 [October 1874]: 674–84).

3. See my discussion of "interloping" in American regional writing in "Universal and Particular: The Local Color Phenomenon Reconsidered," *American Literary Realism: 1870–1910* 12 (Spring 1979): 111–26. Richard Bozman Eaton's remarks about Joseph Frowenfeld in *The Grandissimes* apply equally well to Koppig: "Cable's strategy . . . is to present Joseph as the stranger in the land of Egypt who asks the questions that any reader needs to know the answers to and that could not be plausibly or dramatically presented without a foreigner's presence." Further, "Cable's method insists on the presence of some detached character; economy requires that he be one character; plot that he be integrated into the action. The audience insists that he have personality and therefore opinions relevant to the issues of the novel. He cannot be seen as simply an authorial persona." Eaton argues that this character type is drawn from historical romance. ("George W. Cable and the Historical Romance," *Southern Literary Journal* 8, no. 1 [Fall 1975]: 92)

4. The story's characters live on Dumaine Street. See Lafcadio Hearn, "The Scenes of Cable's Romances," *Century Magazine* 27 (November 1883): 43.

5. Merrill Maguire Skaggs argues that " 'the quadroon balls' " is actually a "euphemistic phrase": by the time the story takes place (1810), these dances featured "institutionalized sexual license." See *The Folk of Southern Fiction* (Athens: University of Georgia Press, 1972), 160.

6. Cable himself indicated the date of the story in a letter to Scribner, Armstrong, and Company (9 February 1878). See Biklé, *Life and Letters,* 58.

7. The text of " 'Tite Poulette" that originally appeared in *Scribner's* says that Koppig wandered "up to Christ Church" (680). When Cable revised the magazine text in the preparation of *Old Creole Days,* he changed this to read "up to the little Protestant affair known as Christ Church" (231). The extra words increase the likelihood that the reader will take note of Koppig's church attendance. Further, the emphasis on Koppig's Protestantism offers yet another obstacle to the young couple's relationship: they have different religions (Protestant and Roman Catholic) in addition to different races and nationalities. However, Cable wisely chose to attend primarily to the racial issue.

8. Philip Butcher, *George W. Cable* (New York: Twayne, 1962), 43.

9. Turner, *A Biography,* 60.

10. Butcher, *George W. Cable,* 44.

11. Charles DeKay, Review, "Cable's *Old Creole Days*," *Scribner's Monthly Magazine* 18 (July 1879): 473.

Chapter 7. Cable's Heart of Darkness

1. Robert Underwood Johnson, *Remembered Yesterdays* (Boston: Little, Brown, 1923), 122.

2. My examples are drawn from the following: Andersen and Sherman,

Scribner's Monthly Magazine 5 (November 1872–April 1873); Headley, ibid. 2 (1871); and Comfort, ibid. 4 (May 1872–October 1872). "'Sieur George" was published in ibid. 6 (October 1873): 739–45.

3. Louis D. Rubin, Jr., *George W. Cable: The Life and Times of a Southern Heretic* (New York: Pegasus, 1969), 50.

4. Lafcadio Hearn, "The Scenes of Cable's Romances," *Century Magazine* 27 (November 1883): 41–42.

5. Cable quotes from "The Lotos-Eaters" in *Madame Delphine* to convey the romance of the heyday of the quadroons in New Orleans society. These women "were indeed the sirens of this land, where it seemed 'always afternoon' " (6).

6. Arlin Turner notes that the *Scribner's* editors "expected a plot with definite complications, suspense, and resolution, and so were hardly prepared for a story achieving its effects through lightness of touch, half-revelation, and suggestion." For the sake of clarity, they advised Cable to add several sentences and a final paragraph (*George W. Cable: A Biography* [Baton Rouge: Louisiana State University Press, 1966], 56–57). Shortly after "'Sieur George" was accepted for publication in *Scribner's*, Richard Watson Gilder wrote to Cable: "Don't forget to be always *clear*— don't weary your reader with trying to remember or discover things—make every sentence as sharp as may be . . ." (29 August 1873, cited in Lucy Leffingwell Cable Biklé, *George W. Cable: His Life and Letters* [New York: Charles Scribner's Sons, 1928], 49).

7. Cable uses George Washington as a standard of honesty in his story "Madame Délicieuse" (1875): "if she could at times do what the infantile Washington said he could not, why, no doubt she and her friends generally looked upon it as a mere question of enterprise" (274).

8. The people of New Orleans, and in particular the Creoles, were angered by Cable's fictional representation of them. In 1885, Richard Watson Gilder asked Grace King why they had taken such an "inimical stand" against Cable and his works. She replied that Cable had " 'stabbed the city in the back . . . in a dastardly way to please the Northern press.' " (Jay B. Hubbell, *The South in American Literature: 1607–1900* [Durham, N.C.: Duke University Press, 1954], 820–21) Hubbell goes on to note that "Many of the Creoles . . . never forgave Cable; indeed, some have not forgiven him even today" (821).

9. Turner, *A Biography*, 57.

10. Claude M. Simpson, ed., *The Local Colorists: American Short Stories, 1857– 1900* (New York: Harper & Brothers, 1960), 256–57.

11. Turner, *A Biography*, 57.

12. Rubin, *Southern Heretic*, 49.

13. Surprisingly, Kjell Ekström, who devotes an entire chapter to the "Possible Literary Influences on *Old Creole Days* and *The Grandissimes*" (chap. 9), does not mention Molière. Ekström notes that Henri Albert Arnaud cites only Hugo, Mérimée, and About as the French writers whom Cable may have read before the writing of *Old Creole Days* (Ekström, *George Washington Cable: A Study of His Early Life and Work,* The American Institute in the University of Upsala, Essays and Studies on American Language and Literature, vol. 10 [Upsala and Cambridge: Harvard University Press, 1950], 91–93; Arnaud, "L'élement français dans l'oeuvre de George Washington Cable," Master's thesis, Louisiana State University, Baton Rouge, 1936).

14. "Et c'est assez pour elle, à vous en bien parler, / De savoir prier Dieu, m'aimer, coudre et filer" (act 1, scene 1, lines 101–2). The translation is by Donald M. Frame, *Tartuffe and Other Plays by Molière* (New York: New American Library, 1967).

15. Brander Matthews, *Molière: His Life and His Works* (New York: Charles Scribner's Sons, 1926), 112.

16. John Palmer, *Molière* (New York: Brewer and Warren, 1930), 251.

17. My remarks about Cable and Molière are not compromised by Cable's well-documented early aversion for the theater. As suggested in the Introduction, being raised in a household that considers acting to be a sinful activity does not necessarily prevent one from studying drama as literature. Furthermore, Cable was quite familiar with French literature, especially the works of Huge, Mérimée, and About (see note 13 above), so it is not unlikely that he had read Molière. It is difficult to believe that the textual similarities between " 'Sieur George" and *L'Ecole des Femmes* are purely coincidental; in fact, Cable's doubts about the morality of the theater would make it very appropriate for him to draw upon an "immoral" play by a controversial playwright in his study of 'Sieur George's moral degeneration. Cable's story would only be enriched by the reader's awareness of Molière.

A final indication that Cable was familiar with Molière is admittedly circumstantial: Cable entitled one of his stories "Jean-ah Poquelin"; Molière's real name was Jean-Baptiste Poquelin.

18. Rubin, *Southern Heretic,* 50.

19. D. H. Lawrence, *Studies in Classic American Literature* (Baltimore: Penguin Books, 1971), 146.

20. Turner, *A Biography,* 4, n. 2.

21. Rubin argues that "it is obvious that the young George Cable was strongly drawn, in spite of himself, to the lolling ways of the Creoles of New Orleans, with their love of ease and their delight in worldly pleasures, their sensual enjoyment of existence in a languorous, semitropical climate. From childhood on, he took great pleasure in the colorful life of the city, the balmy weather, the luxuriant vegetation, the exotic racial mixtures. Cable displayed throughout his life, as Jay B. Hubbell puts it, 'a certain susceptibility to the voluptuous,' and his best fiction derived much of its excitement from the clash between his strong moral disapproval of the Creoles of New Orleans and his keen relish for their ways" (*Southern Heretic,* 26). Cable's championing of civil rights and frequent financial difficulties are discussed in Turner, *A Biography,* chap. 6.

Chapter 8. A Triangle of Transition

1. Cable to Scribner, Armstrong & Co., 9 February 1878, cited in Lucy Leffingwell Cable Biklé, *George W. Cable: His Life and Letters* (New York: Charles Scribner's Sons, 1928), 58.

2. Arlin Turner, *George W. Cable: A Biography* (Baton Rouge: Louisiana State University Press, 1966), 68; Boyesen to Cable, 18 February and 24 November 1877, cited in Arlin Turner, "A Novelist Discovers a Novelist: The Correspondence of H. H. Boyesen and George W. Cable," *Western Humanities Review* 5 (Autumn 1951): 345, 348; Edmund Gosse, Review of *Madame Delphine* [and other stories], *Saturday Review* (London) 52 (20 August 1881): 237–38, cited in Arlin Turner, ed., *Critical Essays on George W. Cable* (Boston: G. K. Hall, 1980), 31; cited in Turner, *A Biography,* 62.

3. Turner, *A Biography,* 62.

4. Etienne de Planchard, " 'Madame Délicieuse': A Political Fable," *Caliban* 2 (1975): 119–26. Although Planchard has anticipated my interpretation of "Madame Délicieuse" as a political allegory structured around a love triangle, his analysis of the story is disappointingly brief and superficial. Further, not all of his arguments

seem tenable. I doubt, for example, that the story was meant to reduce sectional rivalry after the Civil War (125).

5. Grace King discusses the significance of the Eighth of January in *New Orleans: the Place and the People* (New York: Macmillan, 1904), chap. 11, "The Glorious Eighth of January."

6. Merrill Maguire Skaggs, *The Folk of Southern Fiction* (Athens: University of Georgia Press, 1972), 160.

7. Merrill Maguire Skaggs, *Folk of Southern Fiction,* notes that "With his pride in his family and his contempt for labor the Creole of Cable's fiction places a disproportionate emphasis on appearance, especially on keeping up appearances of prosperity . . ." (159). Even after the rejection of his marriage proposal, General Villivicencio continues to visit Madame Délicieuse "to keep up appearances" (285). Significantly, his son had "apparently no idea of how to *show himself* to his social profit" (272, Cable's emphasis).

8. Planchard, "A Political Fable," 122.

9. Lafcadio Hearn discusses the actual buildings mentioned in "Madame Délicieuse" in his "The Scenes of Cable's Romances," *Century Magazine* 27 (November 1883): 44.

10. At the risk of seeming to impose a twentieth-century Freudian reading on a nineteenth-century story, I feel there is at least the possibility that the General fears his son may be homosexual. Such an interpretation would help explain the General's obscure lament, " 'I have more than one burden *here*' " [apparently he touches his heart] (283). Although Cable's fiction does not touch upon homosexuality overtly, he certainly was not averse to probing such aspects of illicit sexuality as incest and miscegenation. Further, Bill Christophersen argues that the two half brothers in "Jean-ah Poquelin" are quite suggestive of "a classic homosexual pair" (" 'Jean-ah Poquelin': Cable's Place in Southern Gothic," *South Dakota Review* 20 [Summer 1982]: 59). This is not to say that Dr. Mossy *is* a homosexual, but that the General may well fear—rightly or not—that that is the source of his son's mild nature. Dr. Mossy's engagement would, of course, quell that fear, while presumably ensuring the continuation of the family's blood line. No wonder the General relinquishes Clarisse so readily to his son.

11. In a letter dated 13 July 1879, Hjalmar H. Boyesen suggested to Cable that "Madame Délicieuse" be placed last: " 'You know reviewers have a way of reading only the first & the last story in a book to judge the rest by these.' " Cable took Boyesen's advice, and beginning with the 1883 edition of *Old Creole Days,* "Madame Délicieuse" has been the final story in the collection (Arlin Turner, "A Novelist Discovers a Novelist: The Correspondence of H. H. Boyeson and George W. Cable," *Western Humanities Review* 5 [Autumn 1951]: 365).

Works Cited

Allen, William Rodney. "Mr. Head and Hawthorne: Allusion and Conversion in Flannery O'Connor's 'The Artificial Nigger.'" *Studies in Short Fiction* 21 (Winter 1984): 17–23.

Asals, Frederick. *Flannery O'Connor: The Imagination of Extremity*. Athens: University of Georgia Press, 1982.

Baskervill, William Malone. "George W. Cable." *Chautauquan* 25 (May 1897): 179–84.

———. *Southern Writers: Biographical and Critical Studies*. Vol. 1. Nashville, 1897. Facsimile reprint. New York: Gordian Press, 1970.

Biklé, Lucy Leffingwell Cable. *George W. Cable: His Life and Letters*. New York: Charles Scribner's Sons, 1928.

The Book of Common Prayer. Greenwich, Conn.: Seabury, 1953.

Butcher, Philip. *George W. Cable*. New York: Twayne, 1962.

———. *George W. Cable: The Northampton Years*. New York: Columbia University Press, 1959.

Cable, George Washington. "After-Thoughts of a Story-Teller." *North American Review* 158 (January 1894): 16–23.

———. *The Creoles of Louisiana*. New York: Charles Scribner's Sons, 1884.

———. *Madame Delphine*. New York: Charles Scribner's Sons, 1896.

———. *Old Creole Days*. New York: Charles Scribner's Sons, 1889.

———. *"Posson Jone'" and Père Raphaël, with a New Word Setting Forth How and Why the Two Tales are One*. New York: Charles Scribner's Sons, 1909.

Campbell, Michael L. "The Negro in Cable's *The Grandissimes*." *Mississippi Quarterly* 27 (Spring 1974): 165–78.

Cardwell, Guy A. *Twins of Genius*. East Lansing: Michigan State University Press, 1953.

Chase, Richard. *The American Novel and Its Tradition*. Garden City, N.Y.: Doubleday, 1957.

Christophersen, Bill. "'Jean-ah Poquelin': Cable's Place in Southern Gothic." *South Dakota Review* 20 (Summer 1982): 55–66.

Clark, William Bedford. "Cable and the Theme of Miscegenation in *Old Creole Days* and *The Grandissimes*." *Mississippi Quarterly* 30 (Fall 1977): 597–609.

Cleman, John. "College Girl Wildness: Nature in the Work of George Washington Cable." *Markham Review* 5 (Winter 1976): 24–30.

DeKay, Charles. "Cable's *Old Creole Days*." *Scribner's Monthly Magazine* 18 (July 1879): 472–73.

Dunbar-Nelson, Alice. "People of Color in Louisiana: Part I." *Journal of Negro History* 1 (1916): 361–76.

Eaton, Richard Bozman. "George W. Cable and the Historical Romance." *Southern Literary Journal* 8 (Fall 1975): 84–94.

Egan, Joseph J. " 'Jean-ah Poquelin': George Washington Cable as Social Critic and Mythic Artist." *Markham Review* 2 (May 1970): [6]–[7].

———. "Lions Rampant: Agricola Fusilier and Bras-Coupé as Antithetical Doubles in *The Grandissimes*." *Southern Quarterly* 18 (Summer 1980): 74–80.

Ekström, Kjell. *George Washington Cable: A Study of His Early Life and Work*. The American Institute in the University of Upsala, Essays and Studies on American Language and Literature, vol. 10. Upsala and Cambridge: Harvard University Press, 1950.

Evans, Oliver. "Melting Pot in the Bayous." *American Heritage* 15 (December 1963): 30–50, 106–7.

Fitzgerald, F. Scott. *Six Tales of the Jazz Age, and Other Stories*. New York: Charles Scribner's Sons, 1960.

Fulweiler, Howard W. "Of Time and the River: 'Ancestral Nonsense' vs. Inherited Guilt in Cable's 'Belles Demoiselles Plantation.' " *Midcontinent American Studies Journal* 7 (Fall 1966): 53–59.

Gosse, Edmund. Review of *Madame Delphine* [and other stories]. *Saturday Review* (London) 52 (20 August 1881): 237–38.

Hawthorne, Nathaniel. *The House of the Seven Gables*. Boston: Houghton Mifflin, 1964.

Hearn, Lafcadio. "The Scenes of Cable's Romances." *Century* 27 (November 1883): 40–47.

Hoffman, Daniel. *Poe Poe Poe Poe Poe Poe Poe*. New York: Avon Books, 1978.

Howells, William Dean. *The Great Modern American Stories*. New York: Boni and Liveright, 1920.

Hubbell, Jay B. *The South in American Literature: 1607–1900*. Durham, N.C.: Duke University Press, 1954.

Hubert, Thomas. "The Gardens of *Old Creole Days*." *Revue de Louisiane / Louisiana Review* 9 (1980): 154–61.

[Johnson, Robert Underwood.] "Cable's 'Madame Delphine.' " *Scribner's Monthly Magazine* 22 (September 1881): 791.

———. *Remembered Yesterdays*. Boston: Little, Brown, 1923.

King, Grace. *New Orleans: The Place and the People*. New York: Macmillan, 1904.

Lawrence, D. H. *Studies in Classic American Literature*. Baltimore: Penguin Books, 1971.

Matthews, Brander. *Molière: His Life and His Works*. New York: Charles Scribner's Sons, 1926.

May, Herbert G., and Metzger, Bruce M., eds. *The New Oxford Annotated Bible*. New York: Oxford University Press, 1973.

Melville, Herman. *Piazza Tales*. Edited by Egbert S. Oliver. New York: Hendricks House, 1948.

Miller, Perry. *Errand into the Wilderness*. Cambridge: Harvard University Press, 1975.

Molière. *Tartuffe and Other Plays by Molière*. Translated by Donald M. Frame. New York: New American Library, 1967.

"My Acquaintance with Cable." *Viestnik Europii* (May 1883). Reprinted in *The Critic* 3 (28 July 1883): 316–17.

Palmer, John. *Molière*. New York: Brewer and Warren, 1930.

Pattee, Fred Lewis. *A History of American Literature Since 1870*. New York: Century, 1915.

Petry, Alice Hall. "Love Story: Mock Courtship in F. Scott Fitzgerald's 'The Jelly-Bean.'" *Arizona Quarterly* 39 (Fall 1983): 251–60.

———. "Universal and Particular: The Local-Color Phenomenon Reconsidered." *American Literary Realism: 1870–1910* 12 (Spring 1979): 111–26.

Planchard, Etienne de. "'Madame Délicieuse': A Political Fable." *Caliban* 2 (1975): 119–26.

Poe, Edgar Allan. *The Complete Tales and Poems of Edgar Allan Poe*. New York: Vintage Books, 1975.

Pugh, Griffith T. "George Washington Cable." *Mississippi Quarterly* 20 (Spring 1967): 69–76.

———. "George W. Cable's Theory and Use of Folk Speech." *Southern Folklore Quarterly* 24 (December 1960): 287–93.

"Recent Novels." *The Nation* 33 (21 July 1881): 54–56.

Review of *Madame Delphine,* by George Washington Cable. *The Critic* 1 (16 July 1881): 190.

Review of *Madame Delphine,* by George Washington Cable. *Literary World* 12 (30 July 1881): 259.

Ringe, Donald A. "The Moral World of Cable's 'Belles Demoiselles Plantation.'" *Mississippi Quarterly* 29 (Winter 1975–76): 83–90.

Rubin, Louis D., Jr. *George W. Cable: The Life and Times of a Southern Heretic*. New York: Pegasus, 1969.

Samway, Patrick, S. J. "Cable's 'Posson Jone'' and 'Père Raphaël': ''Tis a Matt of Conscien'." *Revue de Louisiane / Louisiana Review* 11 (Summer 1982): 61–72.

Simpson, Claude M., ed. *The Local Colorists: American Short Stories, 1857–1900*. New York: Harper & Brothers, 1960.

Skaggs, Merrill Maguire. *The Folk of Southern Fiction*. Athens: University of Georgia Press, 1972.

"Some Recent Novels." *Atlantic Monthly* 88 (December 1901): 845–50.

Stampp, Kenneth M. *The Era of Reconstruction, 1865–1877*. New York: Alfred A. Knopf, 1969.

Stephens, Robert O. "Cable's *Madame Delphine* and the Compromise of 1877." *Southern Literary Journal* 12 (Fall 1979): 79–91.

Stern, Milton R., and Gross, Seymour L., eds. *American Literature Survey: Nation and Region, 1860–1900*. New York: Viking, 1968.

Stone, Edward. "Usher, Poquelin, and Miss Emily: The Progress of Southern Gothic." *Georgia Review* 14 (Winter 1960): 433–43.

Tinker, Edward Larocque. "Cable and the Creoles." *American Literature* 5 (January 1934): 313–26.

Turner, Arlin, ed. *Critical Essays on George W. Cable*. Boston: G. K. Hall, 1980.

———. *George W. Cable: A Biography*. Baton Rouge: Louisiana State University Press, 1966.

———. *Mark Twain and George W. Cable*. East Lansing: Michigan State University Press, 1960.

———. "A Novelist Discovers a Novelist: The Correspondence of H. H. Boyesen and George W. Cable." *Western Humanities Review* 5 (Autumn 1951): 343–72.

Warner, Charles Dudley. "On Mr. Cable's Readings." *Century* 26 (June 1883): 311–12.

Wilson, Edmund. "The Ordeal of George Washington Cable." *The New Yorker* 33 (9 November 1957): 180–96.

———. *Patriotic Gore: Studies in the Literature of the American Civil War*. New York: Farrar, Straus and Giroux, 1977.

Young, Thomas Daniel; Watkins, Floyd C.; and Beatty, Richard Croom, eds. *The Literature of the South*. Glenview, Ill.: Scott, Foresman, 1968.

Zanger, Jules. "The 'Tragic Octoroon' in Pre–Civil War Fiction." *American Quarterly* 18 (Spring 1966): 63–70.

Index